Cases in Management and

Organizational Behavior

Volume 2

Teri C. Tompkins
Pepperdine University

Prentice
Hall

Upper Saddle River, New Jersey 07458

Executive Editor: David Shafer
Editor-in-Chief: Jeff Shelstad
Managing Editor (Editorial): Jennifer Glennon
Editorial Assistant: Kim Marsden
Media Project Manager: Michele Faranda
Marketing Manager: Shannon Moore
Managing Editor (Production): Judy Leale
Production Editor: Keri Jean
Production Assistant: Dianne Falcone
Permissions Coordinator: Suzanne Grappi
Associate Director, Manufacturing: Vinnie Scelta
Production Manager: Arnold Vila
Manufacturing Buyer: Michelle Klein
Design Manager: Pat Smythe
Cover Design: Michael Fruhbeis
Cover Illustration/Photo: Tony Stone
Printer/Binder: Victor Graphics

Credits and acknowledgments borrowed from other sources and reproduced, with permission, in this textbook appear on appropriate page within text.

Pearson Education LTD.
Pearson Education Australia PTY, Limited
Pearson Education Singapore, Pte. Ltd
Pearson Education North Asia Ltd
Pearson Education, Canada, Ltd
Pearson Educación de Mexico, S.A. de C.V.
Pearson Education–Japan
Pearson Education Malaysia, Pte. Ltd

10 9 8 7 6 5 4 3 2 1
ISBN 0-13-089464-8

To my students and colleagues who have made this book possible.

TABLE OF CONTENTS

Preface

I've put this book together to fill a void that I think exists in the field of case teaching. There are not enough intermediate-length cases, especially in organizational behavior and management. Most cases available for the classroom are long, messy cases requiring total commitment to "the case method." There is rarely enough time to review and discuss theory or to include classroom exercises. The alternatives are the short cases at the end of the chapter in the textbook. These cases are usually fictional or gleaned from an article, such as found in the *Wall Street Journal*, not from direct contact with the organization and the people. They require very little thinking from students, with the "problem" and "right answer" clearly drawn from the chapter in question. These end-of-chapter cases provide little challenge for students.

The intermediate-length cases in this book are messy enough that students have to think to analyze them, yet short enough that the instructor can include other teaching methods such as lecture or classroom exercises. The cases are real—the facts of the case have not been altered to make it more illustrative or plausible. Consequently, many of the cases have strong emotional undertones, which draw the students into the case and help them relate to the key characters. Students care about what happens to the people and the organization. Classroom discussion is lively. Students gain mastery of the course content because they have used course-pertinent theories and concepts, along with their own reasoning and relevant experience, to approach genuine organizational problems.

Where Can You Use This Book?

Courses in management or organizational behavior

I've included a detailed matrix referencing each case to 18 different subject chapters. There are numerous cases that would be ideal for human resources management classes, as well. The teaching notes outline questions and teaching plans that are appropriate for undergraduate, graduate, and executive levels.

As a reference book for entire business programs

The range of material in the casebook makes it an ideal reference book for many courses in a bachelor's or M.B.A. program. Cases could be used in courses of management theory, principles of management, organizational behavior, human resources management, communication, negotiation, international management, power and politics, managing change, managing diversity, ethics and social responsibility, entrepreneurship and small business, and managing conflict.

Training programs

The prepared real-life cases and teaching notes meet learning objectives that improve organizational performance. *Organizational development professionals and consultants will find a ready-made source of training materials available in the Casebook and Instructor's Manual of Case Teaching Notes.* Since the cases are intermediate length, the training group can read the case during the session without prior preparation.

Support resources

Fully developed teaching notes including detailed answers, analysis, and an explicit teaching plan for long and short teaching sessions are included in the *Instructor's Manual Case Teaching Notes, Volume 2.* The instructor's manual is indexed by topic so that lesson plans can be quickly organized. Inexperienced case teachers will find it ideal to help them learn how to teach the case. Busy professors, or ones who like to offer spontaneous activities in the classroom, will find the planning in the teaching notes very useful. This high level of support for instructors is unusual for case teaching notes.

Acknowledgments

I owe a special thanks to my dissertation chair, Professor Vijay Sathe, who sent me to gather data in organizations all over the United States and Europe, and asked me to write my first case. When I began teaching organizational behavior as a doctoral student, I was fortunate to select Cohen, Fink, Gadon, and Willets *Effective Behavior in Organizations* as the textbook. These authors taught me about a different style of case teaching. I owe my commitment to fully developed teaching plans to these authors.

I am grateful to Steve Robbins for his mentoring and support over these last three years. He helped my dream of "becoming a writer when I retire" grow into a reality at an earlier age! David Shafer, my editor, has been helpful throughout this entire project. I've also appreciated the support of Jennifer Glennon, Michele Foresta, Judy Leale, Keri Jean, and Kim Marsden at Prentice Hall. My good friends and research colleagues, Katherine R. Rogers, Ann Feyerherm, and Terri Egan, as well as my colleagues at the University of Redlands, have been supportive and encouraging during this intense project. I am grateful to my colleagues at Western Casewriters Association, especially my friend, Anne Lawrence, for her mentoring, and to Asbjorn Osland for his flexibility and support in reviewing and editing 17 student cases for the Western Casewriters 1999 annual workshop.

This work would not have been possible without the excellent work of my two research assistants, Amber Borden and Jonnetta Thomas-Chambers. Their tireless efforts and excellent output kept my spirits up, and improved the quality of this book and teaching note's manual. My mother-in-law, Mittie Lawrence Dick, was especially helpful during the last hours with copy editing. As a member of a generation who was thoroughly schooled in proper grammar, she gave me a lesson on the use of commas that I won't soon forget!

The cases in this book are sensitive, often painful, revealing looks at "moments in time" for the key person in the case. I am grateful to the writers and the subjects in these cases who were willing to share their stories so that students like you could learn from their experience.

Finally, I'd like to thank my family. I have learned to trust God, communicate often, be present in the moment, love openly, and laugh freely because of them. Thank you for your enduring love.

Teri C. Tompkins
Claremont, California

About the Author

Teri C. Tompkins, the eldest in a large family, was born and raised in southern California, where she has enjoyed the rich diversity of people and geography. She received her bachelor of arts and master of science degrees from California State University, Long Beach in not-for-profit management from the Recreation and Leisure Studies department. Her mother often asked her if she was still majoring in "fun." She held several positions in youth agencies including the Girl Scouts of the U.S.A.

In 1983, she quit her job to train and qualify for the 1984 Olympic archery trials. The experience gave her confidence to change careers. She enrolled in the M.B.A. program at The Claremont Graduate University (CGU). As a research assistant for Professor Vijay Sathe, she began researching and writing cases. She subsequently enrolled in the Ph.D. program, and used cases as part of her dissertation research. Upon graduation from CGU, she joined the faculty at The University of Redlands, and became involved in the Western Casewriters Association, where she became president from 1995 to 1996. She is a member of the North American Case Research Association. After receiving tenure at the University of Redlands in 1999, she served as department chair until 2001. She then joined the faculty at Pepperdine University in 2001.

She consults in the areas of team development and learning. Her interests include writing biographies for children, and anything to do with nature including, hiking, biking, and natural science. After delaying parenthood for years, she and her spouse are thoroughly enjoying raising two daughters, ages four and six.

Case Analysis Guideline

There are generally two kinds of cases in this casebook, decision cases and analysis (descriptive) cases. Some cases are both. Decision cases usually require that you identify the problem(s), evaluate solutions, and *decide* what you would do supported by rationale. Analysis cases do not really pose any problems and, therefore, require that you *explain* the behavior in the case.

Your instructor may use cases in class and not expect any preparation from you. At other times, your instructor may request prior preparation before coming to class, such as reading the case, and answering questions. If more extensive preparation is requested or a written assignment is given, these guidelines may be useful.

In decision cases, you may follow a certain "formula" to get the most out of the case. The steps in the formula are a general guideline and may be altered by your instructor based on course objectives. In analysis cases, you seek to explain "why" certain behaviors happened, using appropriate theory, and supplemented with your common sense (developed from life/work experience).

The following steps should guide you in analyzing a case.

Decision Case

1. List the facts.

    Sometimes it helps to list the facts chronologically, or in relationship with key characters, or in some systematic way, to check for areas that are unclear, such as case facts that are ambiguous or differences of opinion if you are working in a group. By listing the facts, you get a sense of the whole of the case. You usually do not turn this part in; it's used to get you oriented.

2. Make inferences about the facts.

    From the facts, what kinds of assumptions do you make? For example, if someone worked eighteen hours a day, seven days a week for five weeks in a row, we could infer several very different reasons why that person worked so many hours. Some might say the person is a "kiss-up," or "disorganized," or "overworked," or "dedicated." It's important to state your inferences so that other people may evaluate whether they agree with you, based on their own interpretation of the facts.

    Inferences are tentative probability statements that may be a basis for deciding on a course of action later on.

3. What is the problem (and why)?

    After identifying the problem(s), try to analyze why they exist. This may lead to an even more critical (or basic) problem. The obvious problem or the problem stated by the character in the case might not be the actual problem that needs solving. It may be a symptom. For example, the direct problem of an employee quitting, when analyzed, might be due to poor communication with her boss, thus suggesting that poor employee relations is a more basic problem. Often there are multiple causes for a problem.

    Is there additional information that you need to analyze the case adequately? A thorough analysis recognizes what information would be gathered, even if you can't actually do it for your analysis.

4. Brainstorm possible solutions to the problem.

    Don't settle for just one or two solutions. Take some time to brainstorm a large quantity of solutions. Following the rules of brainstorming, don't evaluate them until you've generated a sizable amount.

5. For each alternative, list positive and negative consequences.

By evaluating the costs, as well as the benefits, you can possibly modify a potential solution to overcome some of the negative consequences. It is helpful to look for more than one or two consequences. Ask yourself what might happen if we implemented this solution.

6. Make a decision and provide rationale for it.

Making a decision is an important part of the analysis and often forgotten by students in an effort to analyze the problem. Tell what your decision is, the possible consequences, and why you selected the decision. Finally, describe any assumptions you made.

7. What are your "lessons learned" from the case?

What did you learn by analyzing this case? What theoretical concepts were supported or refuted, and why? Are there any new concepts that are suggested by your analysis?

Analysis case

1. List the facts.

2. Make inferences about the facts.

3. Explain the behavior or situation in the case.

Using theory and your own learning, explain *why* events are going on. *Link* the facts from the case with appropriate explanations using such linking phrases as "because of," or "due to," "as a result of," "an example of," "illustrates," or "the following table matches the behavior in the case with the theory." This is the most critical part of a case analysis.

4. Describe your "lessons learned" from the case.

Critical Incident Case Assignment

Purpose of the Assignment

The purpose of this assignment is to link theory and practice. Whether you have lots of work experience or little work experience, it is very likely that you have had experience in organizations. Whether it's sport teams, youth groups, churches or synagogues, friends, schools, or workplaces, you may vividly remember some of the interactions that you have had, probably because there was some emotion tied to them. This assignment challenges you to take a real-life experience that happened to you and link that practical experience to organizational behavior or management theory. Once you have written a narrative case of your experience, you will analyze your behavior, and the behavior of the other key players, based on relevant theory. Then you will develop an action plan that reconnects the theory back to practice. Thus, practice is connected to theory, and theory back to practice.

The assignment has four components. Each component requires a different cache of skills. From this exercise you will develop or improve many of your skills, including creativity, writing, critical thinking, analysis, and editing.

Directions to Complete Assignment

Step 1—Notes to get you started.

*Do step 1 in bullet point; it is not necessary to write complete sentences.
Length: No assigned length but be thorough. You must do all the substeps ("a" through "f" as follows).

(a) Pick a "dilemma or decision" that happened to you at work in which you were puzzled, confused, angry, shocked, hurt, extremely happy, proud, or any strong emotion. If you have limited work experience, choose another setting. Without judging your writing style or grammar, describe the dilemma or decision as completely as you can. Write out as much of the detail as you can remember about the "dilemma" or "decision." Include as many of the senses as you can remember. Use bullet points.

- Sounds
- Sights
- Smells
- Emotions
- Conversations
- Even tastes and textures, if applicable

(b) Think of the other <u>key</u> players. Step back and put yourself in their place. Try to describe the critical incident from their perspective. Write how they might have experienced it, using vivid description. Describe the key players (including yourself) in terms of demographics and psychosocial issues: age, race, education, gender, work experience with the company, leadership style, personality, beliefs, and so on. You may find that you do not need to include all the key players, or you may need to describe more key players.

(c) Using bullet points, outline the history that led to the event and the history after the event. In Step 2, case narrative, you can edit your history to eliminate all but the most important points. The important points should help the class understand the "critical incident" from your perspective and the key players.

(d) Describe the context in which this event happened. That is, for what kind of group or organization did the key players work? How large is the company or group? What kind of business is the company in or what is the purpose of the group?

(e) Decide if you need to include any exhibits to help clarify the case, such as simplified organizational charts, a diagram of the office, or a copy of a letter or memo (you can disguise confidential information or names).

(f) Write an epilogue telling us what actually happened after the critical incident.

Evaluation criteria for Step 1—Notes to get you started

- You did the assignment thoroughly including information in points a, b, c, d, e, and f.
- Your critical incident is focused and can be vividly described. It isn't about a whole year in your life. It is about a key event that may have been preceded by a year in your life (background, history, and contextual information).

Step 2—Narrative

Your assignment is to write an interesting case using the notes from Step 1. The case is in narrative story form; that is, you weave the facts together in a story.
Length: 7 to 12 double-spaced pages.

Look over your notes from Step 1. How can you weave this case together to make it interesting to your classmates? **Write the case in PAST tense. Use third person** (she/he <u>NOT</u> I/we). Describe yourself and others from an objective viewpoint. In other words, don't just tell us that the other person is stupid, mean, and nasty, but **SHOW** us by the person's words and actions. Be truthful; don't make up people or events.

You may disguise the case by changing people's names or other identifying information that you don't want others to know about. You may choose to describe the company in generic terms (e.g., the company produces high-end electronic equipment). You can make up a name, such as Internet Computer Company, or you can use real names of people and the company.

You will be graded on proper grammar and editing. Use 12 point type (preferably Times New Roman, Helvetica, or Ariel). Indent every paragraph five spaces or one tab. Double space between lines but not between paragraphs. Include plenty of subheadings (at least four). Everything should be written in past tense, *including* descriptions of the people and the company, even if this feels awkward. Everything must be written in third person, including descriptions of yourself. If you disguise names, use regular names (not names like Mr. Troublemaker). Avoid names that can be confused with another character (e.g., Al and Albert—change one of their names for clarity to another name, e.g., Chuck).

The easiest way to write a decision-focused case is to:

1. Start out with one paragraph describing you, the decision maker, wondering what to do. For example, "Paula Jones, human resource manager for XYZ Company, sat at her desk wondering what to do. Two of her best warehouse employees had nearly started throwing blows."
2. Write a background section describing the context of the critical incident. This includes information about the company, the group or location, the type of work the key players do, the organizational culture, norms, or quirks, and the product or service. This is usually about three to seven paragraphs.
3. Write a section describing the key players. Depict the psychosocial background of the decision maker and the other key players. Usually this requires one to three paragraphs per

player for the two (or three) major key players and a few sentences for any other key player. Only a few words are usually needed for minor players. Often it is more effective to weave the background about the key players into the story.

4. Describe the critical incident in detail.
5. End with a final paragraph portraying the decision maker as still wondering what to do. Do so **without telling us what the decision maker decided.**
6. Write a part B that tells what the decision maker (you) did.
7. Write an epilogue about what happened to the key players and, if relevant, to the company or group. The epilogue catches us up to the time you wrote the case. If you don't know, catch us up to the time when you lost contact.

Other Ways to Organize Your Case

If you had cooperation from the other key player(s), you could interview the other person(s) and put the case in your own and the other person's words.

Not all cases are decision focused. Some cases (as you will find in this casebook) are descriptive narratives that illustrate theory in an interesting way.

Format of Step 2—Narrative

1. You may use this format for decision-focused or descriptive narrative cases.
2. Title of case narrative (think of a descriptive title).
3. By "your name."
4. Include page numbers at bottom center.
5. Double space.
6. Write an interesting opening that catches the reader's attention.
7. The main body of the story should include enough detail to allow your instructor or a peer review group to understand the problem you faced. It should be interesting to read with dialogue or description that might cause the reader to feel your emotion when the event happened to you.
8. Conclude your case narrative by leaving the reader "hanging," wondering what to do. (You can write what you actually decided or did in a short "B" case).
9. In an **epilogue**, write what is happening to the company and the main players at this moment in time, or the last you heard about them.
10. **Research Methodology:** Describe whether the narrative was based on your own recollections, or any written documents, or interviews with fellow workers, or any other method you used to collect your material.
11. **Industry**: A brief one- or two-sentence description of the industry in which the narrative took place. For example, "small manufacturing plant (160 employees) of high-end electronic equipment; union employees; company disguised/not disguised."

Grading criteria for Step 2—Narrative

- The case describes a critical incident as explained in Step 1.
- The organization of the case is clear and easy to follow. This is a critical criterion.
- It is written in past tense.
- It is written in third person.
- It is not pejorative. You don't tell the reader that the person is stupid, evil, manipulative, and so on. Instead, you illustrate his or her behavior and words, and let the reader draw his or her own conclusions.

- There is enough detail in the case for someone who has no experience with your organization (e.g., the professor) to develop some hypotheses or a list of factors that might explain the behavior. That is, you include enough background information about the company and the key players to help the reader see the context in which the critical incident unfolds, but you don't overwhelm the reader with minutiae.
- It is interesting to read. This is an important criterion.
- The case should be approximately 7 to 12 double-spaced pages, not including the exhibits.
- You include an epilogue.
- You follow the suggested format.

Step 3—Analysis

Your assignment is to analyze the case narrative based on principles of management and organizational behavior theory from your textbook and related readings. Emerging from the issues in your case narrative, choose three topics from the list "Potential topics for case analysis" (or if a relevant topic is not on this list, talk with your instructor). For each chosen topic, write three questions, using the format suggested in the list entitled "Types of Case Questions." Use *three different types* of questions (e.g., cause-and-effect, challenge, and hypothetical questions) within each topic. You may repeat a question type (e.g., hypothetical) in your second or third topic. Label each question (e.g., "hypothetical"). After each question, answer the question thoroughly. Remember to cite appropriate references (author, year, page number), when information is used from your textbook, other books, and articles.

For example, imagine you have to make a decision about how to handle two warehouse employees who nearly fought on the job. First, you would outline the factors that (you think) caused the behavior. Then suppose you found out that one of the employees had a problem with anger, which may be drug related. You could talk about violence in the workplace (from your textbook or reference material). Next, you discover another factor; that is, the two men were from different cultural backgrounds. You could use Hofstede's cultural differences to explain those factors. Then, you would outline possible alternatives of how you might handle the situation. Discuss the positive and negative aspects of each alternative. Finally, you would want to suggest the best course of action to follow based on what you have learned from the organizational behavior theories and your work experience.

Length: 7 to 12 double-spaced pages, and long enough to explain the behavior in the case. This would be difficult to do in less than seven pages, as the case analysis should include at least three topics, with three questions within each topic.

After receiving feedback from your instructor and/or peer review group, using your textbook, and other course materials from management theory, human resources, or organizational behavior, or related courses, make notes about the theory that seems to be most connected to your experience. Focus on *explaining* behavior or suggesting *answers* to a dilemma. Write your analysis by asking yourself *why* the key players responded as they did. Use the theory to explain why or to suggest an action plan.

Format of Step 3—Analysis

1. Analysis of "title of case," followed by your name.
2. Double space, 12 point font (preferably Times-Roman, Helvetica, or Ariel).
3. Include page numbers at bottom center.
4. **Key topics** (the three topics you focused on, and any additional topics you covered).
5. **Abstract:** A 250- to 500-word abstract of your narrative to help the professor remember the case when examining the analysis. An abstract is a summary that briefly tells the reader about the whole case, including case B, if applicable.

6. **Questions and Answers** Topic 1: List the topic (e.g., Motivation or Conflict).
   a. Question 1 (label the type of question, e.g., evaluation or hypothetical—see "types of case questions" attachment).
      i. Answer Question 1.
   b. Question 2 (label type of question, should not be the same type of question as Question 1 or 3 for Topic 1).
      i. Answer Question 2.
   c. Question 3.
      i. Answer Question 3.
7. **Questions and Answers** Topic 2 (same format as Step 6).
8. **Questions and Answers** Topic 3 (same format as Step 6).
9. **References:** Please provide a thorough, APA-style citation for each reference used to support the answers to your questions.
10. **What I learned:** Include a paragraph about what you learned from the analysis of the case narrative.

Grading criteria for Step 3—Analysis

- You select and analyze the most critical factors that influenced the behavior described in your case.
- Your questions follow the format suggested in the "types of case questions" attachment.
- The questions that you asked can be answered by reading your answers to the questions.
- You use relevant theory to explain case factors or to suggest why an action occurred or a decision was made.
- You use at least three different theories, which are not closely related, to explain the behavior described in the case. For example, three motivation theories would count only as one theory.
- You demonstrate your understanding of each theory by how you apply it to your analysis. You use the terms correctly and illustrate the theory appropriately, linking it to case facts.
- Your analysis is clearly written and focused.
- You include a plan of action or a reflection of how you might have done things differently if you knew then what you know now.
- Your action plan considers the pros and cons of various options. Your reflection also considers other paths you might have taken and why you didn't.
- You followed the suggested format.

Step 4—Final version of case

Edit and revise the case narrative and case analysis from Steps 2 and 3 based on student (peer review group) and professor input. Turn in the original copies of Steps 1, 2, and 3 that were edited by the professor and two clean, edited versions based on your revisions. On one of the clean, edited versions please mark the changes you made from the "graded" narrative and the "graded" analysis.

Grading criteria for Step 4—Final Version of Case

- Based on everything you have learned in class to date, rewrite or edit the products of Steps 2 and 3.
- Most narratives of case facts need additional information to support the final analysis and action plan, for there is often missing data in the written case that need to be added. You

would need to take out editorial comments that look like analysis and move them to the analysis section.

- If your analysis included some case facts, then they should have been moved to the case narrative section.
- You included all sections requested by your professor, including the original graded papers from Steps 1, 2, and 3.
- You used three different types of questions for any one topic.
- The narrative and the analysis will be judged on the same criteria as before, except with higher expectations that you know more than you did when you wrote the first draft. Just because you got A's on the other steps does not guarantee you the same grade on your final version. Your instructor assigned grades, on the first part, based on what you knew then. It is assumed that, by the end of the course, you will have learned more and refined your thinking, which should be reflected in the final version. Some students have highlighted, with yellow pen, the areas they particularly want the professor to see in their refinements. Please pick some method to show the changes you have made between your graded narrative and analysis compared to the final version.
- Turn in **two** copies of your final version (including exhibits), one marked up (highlighted) version and one clean copy.

Types of Case Questions

When writing questions, please use a variety of cognitive questions. Try to keep knowledge and comprehension questions to a minimum, unless you use them as a foundation to more complex questions and answers. This is a must for graduate students. Bloom (1956)[1] developed the following system of ordering questions from lower to higher thinking skills.

These types of questions are especially good for <u>descriptive cases</u> or for the <u>theory part of the decision-focused case.</u>

Knowledge skills (remember previously learned material such as definitions, principles, formulas): For example: "Define *contingency design*." "What are the five steps to decision making?"

Comprehension skills (understanding the meaning of remembered material, usually demonstrated by restating or citing examples): "Explain the process of feedback." "Give some examples of groupthink."

Application skills (using information in a new context to solve a problem, answer a question, or perform a task): "How does the concept of Hertzberg's hygiene factors explain the workers' dissatisfaction?" "Given the workers' satisfaction, how would you explain the outcome?"

Analysis skills (breaking a concept into its parts and explaining their interrelationships, distinguishing relevant from extraneous material): "What factors affected the emergent behavior of the team?" "Point out the major arguments Skinner would use to explain this individual's behavior."

Synthesis skills (putting parts together to form a new whole; solving a problem requiring creativity or originality): "How would you organize the leadership of this team in light of new research on emergent leadership?" "How would you overcome barriers to organizational learning?"

Evaluation skills (using a set of criteria to arrive at a reasoned judgment of the value of something): "To what extent does the proposed reorganization resolve the conflict?" "If

---

[1] Bloom, B. S., and others (1956). *Taxonomy of Educational Objectives.* Vol. 1: *Cognitive Domain.* New York: McKay.

bonuses were banned, what would be the implications for the political environment at this firm?"

There are other ways to explore the case by balancing the kinds of questions you ask. The following types of questions are especially good for *decision-focused cases*.

Exploratory questions probe facts and basic knowledge: "What case facts support the theory of Maslow's hierarchy?"

Challenge questions examine assumptions, conclusions, and interpretations: "How else might we account for the behavior of Dr. Sinclair?"

Relational questions ask for comparisons of themes, ideas, or issues: "What premises of Dubinski's are not taken into account by Coleman?"

Diagnostic questions probe motives or causes: "Why did Ferguson not confront his boss about Fester?"

Action questions call for a conclusion or action: "In response to Coleman's ultimatum, what should Sculley do?"

Cause-and-effect questions ask for causal relationships between ideas, actions, or events: "If top management moved this team onto the factory floor, what would happen to its playfulness?"

Hypothetical questions pose a change in the facts or issues: "If the three men did not have similar background factors, would the outcome have been the same?"

Priority questions seek to identify the most important issue: "From all that you have read in this case, what is the most important cause of the conflict?"

Summary questions elicit syntheses: "What themes or lessons have emerged from your analysis of this case?"

Potential Topics for Case Analysis

Managerial Careers, Management Skills
Stages in careers; career anchors; management roles; people skills; entrepreneurship versus management

Decision Making, Creative Problem Solving
Perception; optimizing decision-making model; alternative decision-making models; determinants of attribution; satisficing; intuition; participative decision making; electronic meetings; interacting; brainstorming, nominal, Delphi techniques

Ethics, Diversity
Ethical dilemmas; rationalizations; ethics training; social responsibility; whistle-blowing; work force diversity; gender; comparable worth

Individual Differences
Biographical characteristics; ability; personality; locus of control; learning theories—behavioral, cognitive; values; attitudes

Motivation, Rewards
Theories of motivation; Maslow; Theory X and Theory Y; hygiene factors; high achievers; expectancy theory; underrewarding employees; job satisfaction; MBO; performance-based compensation

Self-Concept, Norms, Roles
Group structure; types of norms; conformity; status; role identity/perception, role expectations and conflict

Critical Incident Case Assignment

Group Dynamics and Work Teams
Identity, cohesiveness, trust; self-managed work teams; virtual teams; committees and task forces

Group Development and Group Interdependence
Phases, competency, group status, differentiation; intergroup relations

Communication and Conflict Management
Key communication skills; process of communication; networks; grapevine; barriers to effective communication; feedback; functional versus dysfunctional conflict; sources of conflict; conflict-handling intentions; benefits and disadvantages of conflict

Power, Influence, Negotiation
Bases and sources of power; power tactics; power in groups and coalitions; empowerment; resource dependency; dependency; distributive/integrative bargaining; third-party negotiation roles

Leadership
What is leadership; trait theories; behavioral theories; Fiedler's contingency model; path-goal theory; situational leadership theory; leader-member exchange theory; charismatic leaders

Organizational Culture, Structure, and Design
Institutionalization; culture characteristics; factors that determine, maintain, and transmit culture; division of labor; unity of command; line/staff authority; span of control; departmentalization; mechanistic and organic structures; Mintzberg's five design configurations; matrix structure; organizations in motion—growth versus decline

Technology and Work Design
Information technology; job redesign; job enrichment

Organizational Learning and Change
Diffusion of knowledge and skills; innovation; stimulants to change; resistance to change; Lewin's model; work stress; stress management strategies; organizational development; OD interventions

Managerial Functions: Planning and Control
The planning process; types of plans—short and long range, strategic and operational; approaches to planning; contingency planning; forecasting; scenarios; benchmarking; budgetary control; types of control—feedforward, concurrent; feedback; internal versus external control; operations management and control

Managing Human Resources
Job analysis; interviewing in selection; performance simulation versus written tests; performance evaluation; training and development programs

Productivity: Individual, Group, and System
Absence rates; turnover; job fit; job analysis; role perception and satisfaction; socialization; reducing ambiguity; matching structure to mission

Globalization and Stakeholders
Multinational corporations; environmental influences—economic, legal, political, and educational; strategies for international business; cultural dimensions; international management; cases in other countries beyond the United States and Canada (with relevant background of the country); union-management interface

Opportunity for Publication

About 50 percent of the cases published in this casebook were written by students like yourself. If you have written an interesting case and analysis, please consider submitting it for the next edition of *Cases in Organizational Behavior and Management.* If you have written a case situated in a country other than the United States. or Canada, you will have an immediate opportunity for publishing in the *International Casebook*. Please include all the information suggested in the format for the case narrative and analysis.

      It is preferred that you submit an e-mail attachment of your final edited version (case narrative and analysis) along with contact information (phones, address, e-mail address, school or work affiliations). Save as a Word document for Windows. Submit to Teri.Tompkins@pepperdine.edu.

      We will contact you within a day or two to acknowledge receipt. If you do not receive confirmation within three weeks, please resubmit your e-mail asking if your submission was received. **Or** submit an IBM-formatted disk copy and printed version of your final edited version (including the case narrative and analysis with questions and answers). **Please include all your contact information** (phone, e-mail, address, school or work affiliations).

      Submissions sent by postal or overnight service should be addressed to:

        Professor Teri C. Tompkins
        Submission to *Cases in Organizational Behavior and Management, 2nd edition*
        OR *International Casebook*
        Graziadio School of Business and Management
        Department of Management
        Pepperdine University Plaza
        400 Corporate Pointe, Suite 300
        Culver City, CA 90230
        USA

Matrix of Cases and Subjects

P = Primary Topic with Teaching Plan
X = Topic, but no teaching plan

Case Title	Page Number	1. Managerial Careers, Management Skills	2. Decision Making, Creative Problem Solving	3. Ethics, Diversity	4. Individual Differences	5. Motivation, Rewards	6. Self-Concept, Norms, Roles	7. Group Dynamics and Work Teams	8. Group Development and Interdependence	9. Communication and Conflict Management	10. Power, Influence, Negotiation	11. Leadership	12. Organizational Culture, Structure, and Design	13. Technology and Work Design	14. Organizational Learning and Change	15. Managerial Functions: Planning and Control	16. Managing Human Resources	17. Productivity: Individual, Group, System	18. Globalization and Stakeholders
A Selfish Request in Japan	1	X	X	X		X				X	P						X		P
Angry Branch Manager	6		P	P	P	X	P			X									
Café Latte, LLC	11			P	P											P			
Changing Quotas	15		P			P	X			P									
Computer Services Team at AVIONICS	20							P		X		P	P		X	X		X	
Cost and Scheduling Team at AVIONICS	24	X						P	P	X	P	P			X	X		X	
Groupware Fiasco	31		P					X	P					X					
Incident on the USS Whitney	35						P					P	P			P			
Insubordination or Unclear Loyalties?	39	X	P								P	P	P						
Leading TQM in Panama	43										P	P	P		P			X	P
Negotiating Work Hours	48					P		X		P	P								
Preferential Treatment?	55			P		P				X	P						P		
Reputation in Jeopardy	58									P	X		P		X			X	X
Richard Prichard and the Federal Triad Programs	63					P	X											X	
Saving Private Ryan Video Case: Classic Leadership Models	69											P							
The Safety Memo	72		P	P						P	P	P	P					X	
The Volunteer	79					P					P	X				P			
Then There Was One	85	P																	
Unprofessional Conduct	89	P				X				X							P		
Violence at the United States Postal Service	92	P		X	X	X				X	X		P	X			P	X	
When Worlds Collide	102																		P

CASES

A Selfish Request in Japan

by Tobias M. Lee

PART A

In 1995, Toby Lee, an American, decided to attend the Drucker School of Management in Claremont, California. At that time, he was employed as an English teacher in Yokohama, Japan, at one of the largest language school chains in the country. The lone obstacle standing between him and his trip to Claremont was the dreaded GMAT. The date of the GMAT was Saturday, October 19, 1995. Toby's contract stipulated that he work from Tuesday through Saturday. To make matters worse, his company, NOGI, was threatening to terminate his employment if he took the test. Toby had a problem.

Toby Lee's Dreams

At 22 years of age and fresh out of college, Toby went to Japan with the intent of staying for two years and then returning to business school. His job with NOGI secured him a visa and allowed him to reside in Japan while he pursued his first love, martial arts. As a member of the U.S. Junior Olympic taekwondo team, Toby befriended a Japanese competitor named Nobiyuki. The two had kept in touch over the years and always talked about competing as professional fighters some day and owning a studio together. When Toby arrived in Japan on June 20, 1995, those dreams became a reality. The Kawasaki Budokan (school name) was established a few months later, which became Japan's premier professional fighting organization. Tokiona had two new fighters. Little did Toby know that his biggest fight would not be in the ring.

NOGI English Language School

In July 1995, during his first month as an English teacher and three months prior to the test date of October 1995, Toby submitted a written request to NOGI's head office for a day off to take the GMAT. After communicating his desire to attend business school and the importance of this test to his manager, Yuko Nakamura, he was instructed to direct all correspondence to the head office concerning this matter. Ms. Nakamura had no authorization to allow staff members at her school to take days off.

The second largest English school chain in the country, NOGI boasted over 350 schools throughout Japan. Each school averaged from two to four American teachers who had been hired on a one-year contract in America. The rest of the staff was entirely Japanese. Although the interview process to secure a job at NOGI was rigorous, nothing can properly prepare an American for immersion into Japanese culture. Indeed, many NOGI teachers had broken their contract and returned home because of the very different lifestyle that occurs in the land of the rising sun. For this reason, NOGI managers were very skeptical of their American staff and watched them carefully to ensure they were taking their jobs seriously and not out for a free vacation.

Americans working for NOGI had a contract that spelled out their relationship with NOGI, specifying such issues as mandated specific dress codes (including unacceptable colors) and hairstyles. The attempt here was to present a standard appearance of professionalism and not

The author wishes to thank Jonnetta Thomas-Chambers for her thoughtful comments and editing.

to distinguish oneself from other teachers. It also included numerous regulations that required American teachers to participate in non-work-related activities on unscheduled workdays.

The Japanese corporate system is very rigid and structured. NOGI was no different. Extremely centralized and top-down, any problem at one of the local schools was documented and dealt with at the corporate headquarters. Local managers were instructed to handle personal problems but to direct all professional matters to the head office. Meetings, reports, and faxes were an important and time-consuming part of the business process at NOGI.

Hisami Davies was the vice president of human resources at NOGI's corporate headquarters and the next person Toby would talk to concerning his day off. His first conversation with her began a week before his test date. Up until that time he had assumed that his day off had been granted. His name had been removed from the teaching schedule that week, indicating that preparations for his absence had been made. He often asked Ms. Nakamura and his head teacher, Yoko Yamashina, whether or not they had heard anything. They always replied that they didn't know and hadn't heard.

Tuesday Through Saturday Without Exception

Ms. Davies, however, did know and she told Toby that his request had been denied. NOGI could not allow employees to take a personal day off at their discretion because it endangered the efficient operation of their business. Ms. Davies told him that his contract required him to work from Tuesday through Saturday without exception. The only exceptions were defined as attending a wedding or funeral for direct family members. In these cases (except funerals), written proof from the families had to be submitted one month in advance for approval. NOGI considered Toby's request a selfish one. It was a personal day that, from the company's perspective, was equivalent to spending the day playing baseball because both activities failed to add value to the corporation.

Toby argued that this test was for the betterment of his future and that it was only offered on Saturdays. He believed that he had provided them sufficient time to accommodate his request and that notifying him of their decision a week before his test was unprofessional. NOGI had a division of emergency teachers whose sole purpose was to cover for other teachers who were sick. Toby argued that he could have just called in sick and that this would have been deemed a legitimate absence. Ms. Davies reminded him that the students were paying a lot of money to be taught by him and having another teacher provided them with a lesser service. She urged him to think of the team and not just himself. He was told that being absent that Saturday would result in serious disciplinary actions.

Meeting with NOGI Management

Understanding where the head office stood on this issue, Toby met with Ms. Nakamura and Ms. Yamashina for their opinions. As the manager and head teacher, they occupied the two most powerful positions at his local school.

Ms. Nakamura had been the manager at NOGI Tsurumi (city name of the local school) for over two years and had been an assistant manager before that for another two. At only 27 years of age, she was one of the younger managers in the company but highly regarded for her hard work ethic and ability to consistently achieve profits. The first one to arrive at work and the last one to leave, Ms. Nakamura was determined to climb the corporate ladder at NOGI. The path to seniority at NOGI, as with most Japanese companies, favored men, as the corporate ladder was built with rungs difficult for women to climb. Maintaining strong relationships with her regional manager, Mr. Miyake, Ms. Nakamura operated her school directly by the book and did not make exceptions. She strongly believed in the centralized management system that NOGI practiced because it maximized order, efficiency, and structure. Ms. Nakamura was highly ethical and procedural in her management style. Objectivity was a constant principle throughout her relations with the various employees, Japanese and American. Despite the difficulty in developing a personal relationship with her, no one could discount her fairness.

Ms. Yamashina had been the head teacher at NOGI Tsurumi for four years, starting at the exact same time as Ms. Nakamura. The two were also the same in age but their similarities stopped there. Ms. Yamashina had spent her college years in America and was heavily influenced by American culture. Trendy and fashionable, Ms. Yamashina was utterly the antithesis of the very conservative and traditional Ms. Nakamura. She had a strong desire to be liked and this was evident in her inconsistent leadership style. Favorable to those on whom she wished to make a good impression, Ms. Yamashina often defended the American staff and felt empowered by their support. As part of the constant power struggle between herself and Ms. Nakamura, the American troops usually marched for Ms. Yamashina. As the intermediary to Japanese management, Ms. Yamashina was often torn between the American ideology and her native coworker's traditional mentality.

Ms. Nakamura and Ms. Yamashina asked Toby to summarize his phone conversation with Ms. Davies in full detail. They took many notes and often consulted each other in Japanese. The tone of the meeting turned very serious as Ms. Nakamura asked Toby if he understood the employee contract that he had signed. He reported that he did and then went on to reiterate the argument that he gave Ms. Davies. Ms. Yamashina, usually very supportive and understanding, adopted an unusually corporate demeanor and told him that customer satisfaction was critical to the school's success. The central theme of their argument boiled down to "What about the students?"

As Toby listened to their argument he couldn't help but think, "What about me?" As a contracted employee, Toby realized that teaching English was not a career move for him. However, he also realized that he had certain responsibilities to his job and to his coworkers. He had hoped to alleviate the burden on his coworkers by allowing sufficient time for the school to make the appropriate arrangements for a substitute teacher. He was willing to work another day to compensate for his day off and strove to reach a compromise. Ms. Nakamura and Ms. Yamashina offered no display of emotional understanding but stood by the decision of the corporate head office. They wouldn't comment on what would happen if Toby intentionally missed work that Saturday to take the GMAT and remained somewhat indifferent to the whole situation. Toby was very disturbed by the either-or situation and left work that night disappointed, confused, and upset.

As a first-generation Chinese American, Toby had been raised in a very traditional Asian household. Strict adherence to authority and conformity were issues he had been continually exposed to as a child and ones he was rather partial to as an adult. But he wondered if the concept of playing by the rules was the relevant issue in this case. He thought, "How can I play the game when the rules are inherently wrong?"

[Please do not read Part B until instructed to do so by your instructor.]

A Selfish Request in Japan (B)

After his phone call with Ms. Davies and his meeting with Ms. Nakamura and Ms. Yamashina, Toby was very upset. He had prepared for the GMAT over the past three months and filed all the appropriate paperwork to take the test in Japan. He believed that he had acted extremely professionally with respect to the bureaucratic process at NOGI. Only four months into his job, which he was thoroughly enjoying, he faced possible termination. His martial arts studio was growing and his fighting career had also been very successful. Financially, the English teaching job was not a necessity and Tokiona, the fighting organization, was willing to sponsor his visa. Still he preferred to stay with the school. Toby believed that NOGI's actions were illegal.

Personal Days in Japan

After his initial request in July went unanswered for a month by NOGI's head office and local management, Toby began doing research about personal days allotted to foreign employees. According to Japanese law, all foreign employees were allowed seven personal days per year (considering that the employee worked at least 75 percent of that year) to be taken at their discretion. Management could disallow this request if the absence of that employee endangered the operation of the business. Within the context of his situation, Toby knew that NOGI was acting improperly and that he was legally entitled to take this personal day off. He had not raised this issue with Ms. Davies, Ms. Yamashina, or Ms. Nakamura yet because he wanted to have sufficient support once talks of legality ensued.

The very next day, after meeting with NOGI management, Toby made an appointment at the Tokyo South General Workers Union. He met with Jim Crawford, the vice president, who was also a lawyer and an American who had worked in Japan for the past eight years. Mr. Crawford had also been an English teacher and understood the "unusual" stipulations and clauses that Japanese companies often imposed on their American employees. NOGI had two contracts, one for Japanese and one for Americans. They were fundamentally different. Among other differences, the Japanese teaching contract at NOGI was more flexible concerning personal days. Japanese employees requesting personal days did not need to submit their request to the head office as local Japanese managers could approve their request. After careful examination of the NOGI employee contract for Americans, Mr. Crawford was confident that they had a strong case. He urged Toby to consider starting a union for NOGI teachers so that the head office didn't try to appease his request without holding itself responsible to the thousands of other American teachers throughout the country.

Surprise Support

That night, Toby began making calls to other teachers to gain support. Only 10 members were needed for an official union to be established in Japan. The establishment of the union happened very quickly and rather easily. Throughout the first three months of his employment at NOGI, Toby had interacted with many other NOGI teachers who expressed similar feelings of dissatisfaction with corporate policies. Toby was rather surprised at the support he received as he made his initial phone calls. Indeed, he did not even make all the phone calls. Many of the NOGI teachers he contacted volunteered to contact other NOGI teachers they knew to garner support.

A few days later Toby received a phone call from Ms. Davies. She asked him again if he was planning to report to work that Saturday. Toby responded that he intended to take the GMAT and had already informed his manager so that she could make appropriate accommodations on that day. Ms. Davies voiced her displeasure and told Toby that the regional manager, Mr. Miyake, wanted to meet with him the next day to further discuss the matter.

Toby felt somewhat nervous meeting with Mr. Miyake at their corporate headquarters. A senior executive in the company, Mr. Miyake was a very traditional and serious Japanese businessman. Toby knew that he would try and intimidate him into working that Saturday or threaten him with some form of disciplinary action. Toby also knew that he was legally entitled to this day off and asked Mr. Crawford to accompany him for legal support.

As the two entered the building, the receptionist was very surprised to see that Toby had a guest. The level of surprise intensified as Mr. Miyake was introduced to Toby's guest, the vice president of the Tokyo South General Workers Union. Immediately the talks turned very serious as Mr. Crawford articulated the illegalities of the employee contract. Mr. Miyake would not admit any wrongdoing and said that the company's attorney would need to speak with him directly. Periodically, Mr. Miyake would speak directly to Toby and attempted to persuade his actions for the sake of the company.

Terry Allen, the head trainer for foreign teachers, joined the meeting a bit later. A 10-year veteran in Japan, Terry attempted to sympathize with Toby while gradually reinforcing the company's argument. Mr. Allen affirmed the difficulties and challenges Americans faced, working and living in Japan. While his demeanor appeared sympathetic, his statements continuously revolved around the commitment to the company and the need to understand the dangerous risk this precedent would set. If Toby did this, then the thousands of other American teachers might also do this. Toby stuck to his argument and knew that it was grounded in principle and law. At the end of the heated discussion, Toby and Mr. Crawford were confident that Mr. Miyake and Mr. Allen realized the incorrect stance their company had taken. Mr. Miyake acknowledged that Toby would not be present for work that Saturday and that actions taken by NOGI would come at a later date.

NOGI's Response

The day before the test, Toby met again with Ms. Nakamura and Ms. Yamashina. They told him that the head office was aware of his intentions and that his wages would be withheld for that day. They did ask him to return to school after his test so that he could teach one private lesson class for 40 minutes. Although his commute to work was over an hour each way, Toby conceded to this request as a demonstration of his intent to compromise. Ms. Yamashina was visibly upset at Toby's decision, especially since she had to take an additional class that day. Ms. Nakamura remained indifferent, merely following the orders given by Mr. Miyake. They were both, however, very curious about the NOGI Teacher's Union that had been established that morning as nine coworkers and Toby marched into the union office, paid their membership fees, and established a forum where employee rights could be discussed. Toby did not comment on the union directly but explained his desire to be treated fairly and legally.

Challenging authority is a concept that the majority of Japanese neither practice nor respect. This ideology is even more evident in the workplace where employees traditionally act without question. Acting against the consensus is often viewed as selfish and disrespectful. Toby's request to take a personal day off for the GMAT, his decision to seek professional help in the form of the Tokyo General Workers Union, and his part in establishing NOGI's first Teachers Union were all being seen as such.

On October 15, 1995, Toby sat down to take the GMAT. He had no idea that his test preparation would include a lesson in Japanese corporate hierarchy, employment laws, and coworker relations. After suffering through four hours of mathematical equations and argumentative questions, he returned to work and saw Ms. Yamashina in the lobby. She did not greet him, did not inquire about his test, and did not look at him. Ms. Nakamura did say "hello," and then reminded him to thank his coworkers for taking additional classes on his behalf. Clearly, this Saturday, and its significance, was as undesirable for Toby's coworkers as it was for him.

The next week, Terry Allen, the head trainer at NOGI, visited NOGI Tsurumi to meet with Toby. His attitude this time was much different, and it began with an apology. He acknowledged the stringent policies in the employee handbook and reported to Toby that his wages would be compensated for that Saturday. He also told Toby that NOGI was currently working to revise its employee contracts. A year and a half later, that finally materialized.

Angry Branch Manager

by Joe Underwood

On Friday, October 16, 1999, one of the human resources representatives at Calwest Mortgage Company, Joe Underwood, was preparing to go to lunch when his telephone rang. Instead of sending the call to his voice mail, as his rumbling stomach urged him to do, Joe went ahead and answered the telephone. Nearly two hours later, he hung up the telephone and leaned back in his chair, virtually forgetting that he had failed to get lunch. He decided to discuss the call with Stephanie Lawson, the human resources manager. As he entered her office and shut the door, he sat down and simply said, "There's trouble brewing in Manhattan Beach again. It looks like we may have to conduct the investigation this time."

Joe continued to tell Stephanie about the telephone call. Sal, an account executive at the Manhattan Beach office, had called human resources from his own home because he decided that he no longer felt safe in the office. He went on to describe a history of emotional and physical abuse by Henry, his branch manager. Henry, Sal explained, screamed and cursed at his associates on a daily basis. Sal contended that Henry would "speak right in my ear." He also suggested that Henry would raise his voice frequently for no real reason, which Sal found very threatening. Sal explained that Henry often drove his associates to tears. For example, sometimes when Henry got angry, he would shove associates and invade their personal space. According to Sal, Henry threatened to "take them all down with him" if any of his associates ever reported him to human resources. After Joe described the call, Stephanie shook her head and said, in a soft, monotone voice, "I thought that situation was taken care of. Okay, get prepared. We are going down to Manhattan Beach on Monday."

The Organization

Calwest Mortgage Company was the largest specialty-lending mortgage company in the nation to offer mortgage-backed loans to individuals who were unable to get loans from other institutions because of past credit problems, large debt, or lack of provable income. Calwest, a privately held organization, quickly outpaced all of its competitors in growth and profitability. In 1995, while other mortgage companies laid off their employees, Calwest tripled in growth for three consecutive years, securing 170 branches throughout the United States thereafter. This growth was primarily due to its ability to adapt. During this growth period, the organization changed its loan product packages (e.g., fixed rate, variable rate, loan length, etc.) in response to market demands, while its competitors continued marketing products that returned little profit.

Calwest was a sales-driven organization. Eighty-five percent of the staff was comprised of account executives and loan origination officers, whose primary duty was to sell the loan package-of-the-month to customers in their local areas. The other 15 percent of the staff were comprised of line managers and support staff. A small base salary and commission compensated everyone except the support staff. Due to the boom in business at that time, the commissions could get quite large. For example, the average account executive made over $50,000 and the average branch manager made over $100,000.

Calwest had a policy of promoting from within. Promotion to branch manager was usually based on previous performance as an account executive. As such, new branch managers typically had very good sales skills but little management experience. Calwest also had a policy of quickly firing anyone whose performance did not meet the organization's standards. Specifically, if an associate's performance lacked for three months, the associate was terminated or demoted. Although this policy was unwritten, associates at every level understood it.

Whether promoted from within or hired from outside the organization, new managers received very little training. Within the first three months in their new position, branch managers would attend a one-week training session at the corporate office. The majority of the training sessions taught the managers how to sell loans. The human resources session, which suggested different management techniques, lasted only an hour. All other management knowledge had to be learned on the job or was taught by the area manager. Of course, the area managers never received any more management training than the branch managers did.

Key Players

Stephanie Lawson, human resources manager, was a 28-year-old, Caucasian female who had been with Calwest for seven years in an employee relations capacity and three years in a HR manager capacity. She tended to be company oriented in her approach to employee issues. As such, upper management greatly respected her.

Joe Underwood, human resources representative, was a 30-year-old, Caucasian male who had been with Calwest for six months as a recruiter and eight months as a HR rep. Before Calwest, he had three years of banking and mortgage experience, although none of the experience was HR related. He was perceived by upper management as an educated (M.A. in cognitive psychology and currently working on an M.A. in HR) and motivated associate. He was generally thought of as popular with the employees, though he typically mirrored Stephanie's company-oriented approach.

Michael Griffin, regional manager, was a 36-year-old, African American male who had been with Calwest for eleven years, and in his current position for three years. He had begun his career at Calwest as an account executive and had worked his way through the ranks until he had been promoted to the regional manager position. He was perceived as a supportive manager by his associates and approached his job with a no-nonsense attitude.

Henry Starks, branch manager, was an African American male who had been with Calwest for two years. He had four years of mortgage experience, though no previous management experience. He was described by peers as short in stature with a big man's attitude. He was self-described as somewhat paranoid because "as a black man in this industry, you always gotta' watch out." From the very beginning of Henry's employment, he had the preconception that he had to be very careful at Calwest because he was African American. For example, he tape-recorded conversations that he had with his employees, senior management, and human resources. Typically, he tape-recorded the conversations without the knowledge or consent of the person(s) being recorded. He also told his employees that management heavily scrutinized him because they were always looking for ways to terminate him as "they had all the other black managers."

Sal Khan, account executive, was a Middle Eastern male who had been with Calwest for one year as an account executive. He was very excitable and emotional. He was a strong Henry supporter during previous HR investigations.

The Manhattan Beach Branch

In the last two years, the Manhattan Beach branch had employed three different managers. Before Henry, the other two managers had both been demoted for lack of productivity. Five months prior to Sal's telephone call, Henry had accepted his position as manager of the branch. Henry sat down with his employees and taught them how to sell loans, and within the first few months, the branch started to perform well. Although most of the associates had rarely made commissions before Henry became their manager, within a month they began to average $900 per month in commission checks. A few associates even doubled their monthly salaries.

During Henry's second month as manager, human resources received a call from one of his associates who complained about disparate treatment in the branch and, in general, Henry's management style. When human resources contacted the regional and area managers for the Manhattan Beach branch, the area manager conducted a quick investigation but was unable to corroborate the associate's story. However, it was discovered that Henry had conducted questionable business practices, such as bait 'n' switch and routinely taping his conversations with other associates without their consent. The area manager decided to counsel Henry but did not put the counseling in writing. The area manager also transferred the associate who had alleged the problems to another branch the next day without telling the other associates why this particular associate was leaving.

Two weeks later, another associate called with similar complaints. This person also alleged that Henry had cursed at customers and had made a gender slur when talking with her. Michael Griffin, the regional manager, suspended the associate with pay and conducted a more thorough investigation. Michael conducted the investigation as impartially as possible. Two other associates, friends of the one who complained, agreed that there were management issues. However, they were unable to agree as to what the issues were or corroborate the gender slur. Prior to these allegations, all three associates had recently been placed on 60-day warnings for low productivity. The remaining six associates all agreed that Henry was a good manager and wrote written statements on his behalf. However, Henry was making them more money than they had ever made before and, as one employee stated during the second interview, "I had just made a $1,200 commission check. Would you have ratted him out?" Michael decided that the preponderance of the evidence suggested that Henry's management style was sufficient—and human resources agreed. In addition, although Michael and HR suggested that Henry be written up directly to the area manager, Henry was never disciplined. The associate who called HR returned to work for a short time but was soon offered a transfer to a more lucrative position closer to her home. HR never followed up with the employees after the investigation to make sure that they were still comfortable with the culture within the branch.

Within the next four months, the branch experienced a tremendous turnover rate of 80 percent compared to its normal turnover rate of 56 percent. The increase in turnover was attributed to several reasons.

- Henry terminated two associates for productivity during the fourth month of his employment as branch manager. Although these two employees had been the worst two producers in the branch, the other employees were not performing significantly better. In fact, Henry's production goals were high compared to the average Calwest branch manager's. Instead of facing possible termination, they may have decided to disclose Henry's behavior in hopes of getting a new manager or securing a transfer for themselves.
- The two associates who had recently called human resources voluntarily quit.
- The two associates who had voiced that management issues existed voluntarily transferred to other branches.
- Three more associates transferred to other Calwest branches as well.

The area manager relished the changes and asserted that the branch could "get a fresh start with Henry leading the team." A couple of weeks after that, the telephone call from Sal prompted the human resources investigation.

The Investigation

The investigation was conducted at the Manhattan Beach office. By the time Stephanie and Joe arrived from the corporate office, Michael, the regional manager, had already told Henry to go home for the rest of the day. Stephanie and Joe had already interviewed Henry over the telephone the day before. Michael, too, had separately interviewed Henry at his branch behind closed doors. Henry consistently alleged that he never cursed or exhibited physically or mentally threatening behavior. Henry then contended that Sal had recently expressed anger toward him because he made Sal split a commission bonus with another associate. Sal believed that he had been the primary reason for the origination of the loan and should receive the full commission.

Henry asserted that Sal had been very happy with his management style prior to their confrontation and believed the confrontation prompted Sal's telephone call to human resources.

When Joe and Stephanie arrived at the Manhattan Beach office, they asked Michael to join them in an empty conference room. They called Sal and asked him to come to the branch. When he joined them, the investigation officially began. Stephanie informed each witness that this was an official investigation and that Calwest had a strict policy against retaliation. She then proceeded to lead the investigation. Occasionally, Joe or Michael would ask a clarifying question. Each witness was given ample time to answer each question and was asked, at the end of the questioning period, to add anything that they thought might be helpful. They were also allowed to ask any questions they wanted, although not all of them were answered for reasons of confidentiality.

Sal was the first witness. He did verify Henry's story that he believed that the commision had been split unfairly with another associate. However, he claimed that this was simply one of many unfair management practices. The other three associates who were present were also interviewed. One customer also agreed to be interviewed. This customer was chosen because Sal alleged that Henry had grossly mistreated her in a recent loan closing.

Stephanie was a very skilled investigator, and she would often ask apparently innocuous questions that would be very telling by the end of the conversation. Because of this, she was able to draw more information out of the employees than they initially wanted to disclose.

Employees said they were initially surprised when they discovered that he taped every formal conversation that he had with them. Although they were not entirely comfortable with being taped, they viewed the act as one of Henry's quirks and decided that they could live with it. Employees also stated that Henry made anti-corporation statements, such as "HR is like the Gestapo and can't be trusted." Henry told his employees that they would never need to speak to HR or any other corporate entity because he would take care of them by judiciously handling any of their issues.

One of the major concerns for three of the four interviewed employees was Henry's aggressive approach to management. They suggested that Henry would be very nice and easygoing one minute but extremely heated the next minute. Whenever he spoke to them about their job performance, he would stand very close to them and raise his voice often. They found this behavior to be very intimidating and often frightening. In fact, they suggested that because he grew so angry so quickly and easily they were afraid that he might be prone to greater violent outbursts if further provoked. Three of the employees disclosed that Henry had threatened them with retaliation should they admit any management wrongdoing to the regional manager.

After interviewing everyone, the three investigators looked over their notes and discussed the various issues. They took turns describing their perceptions of each person and the facts that they presented. They finally agreed on the following issues.

The Issues

Issue 1 - Physical abuse: Sal asserted that Henry had pushed his associates on several occasions. No other associates verified this assertion; however, one associate did claim that she thought that Henry was capable of violence, and worried that he would harm her children. In addition, the customer who was interviewed commented that she hoped Henry "did not come to her house with an axe in hand."

Issue 2 - Mental abuse: Sal also asserted that Henry screamed and yelled at his associates. He claimed that Henry often cursed at and demeaned his associates. Two of the other associates agreed that he yelled when angry but also pointed out that he was very congenial and fun when he was happy. The third associate claimed that she had never heard him yell during the three weeks she worked in the branch. None of the associates verified that Henry cursed in the office.

Issue 3 - Micromanagement: Sal asserted that Henry constantly watched and criticized his every move. He also claimed that Henry would have six or more impromptu meetings with him throughout the day for status updates. Sal suggested that these meetings interfered with his ability to perform his job function adequately. Two of the three associates agreed that Henry micromanaged them, too, but they did not consider this management style an impediment to their job functions.

Issue 4 - Intimidation and retaliation: Sal asserted that Henry was very intimidating and had threatened retaliation if he ever approached Michael or human resources. Two of the other associates did verify this claim. Furthermore, they both independently suggested that Henry had coerced them to alter their written testimonies during the previous investigation that had been conducted by Michael.

Issue 5 - Lack of written performance issues: Although Henry had received several counseling sessions by his previous area manager, he had never received any written notice. Per Calwest policy, they rarely terminated an associate without at least one piece of previously written documentation.

Issue 6 - Race discrimination: Calwest was already involved in a race discrimination issue in another area of the United States. Although the two cases were unrelated, Stephanie noted that Henry had previously suggested that his area manager had counseled him because "he was black." She was, therefore, afraid that another race claim could add unneeded exposure to the previous race claim. In actuality, although there were only seven African American managers out of 178 total managers in the sales force at Calwest (over 60 percent of the rest of the managerial force was some other minority status), only one of the African American managers was currently on a performance-issued action plan. Three of the seven were top producers and were very highly regarded by top management. Michael Griffin, an African American, was a regional manager, which was one of the top management positions in the whole company.

Issue 7 - Tape recordings: Michael noted that it was believed that Henry would tape-record his conversations with other Calwest associates without telling them. In this case, he was afraid that any recordings of the area manager, who had recently been demoted as a result of questionable business practices, could be potentially damaging to the company's reputation.

The Decision

The issues had been outlined. The investigation was now complete. The three investigators now had to unanimously decide what to do about Henry.

Cafe Latte, LLC (A)

by Kim Hui

Cynthia Chan, partner of Cafe Latte, LLC, stormed out of the restaurant and slowly exhaled. She was greatly disturbed by the incident she had just encountered and needed to walk off some of her anger and overwhelming sense of frustration. She was still visibly angry, her jaw and fists clenched. Just minutes before, she had walked into a barrage of angry accusations by her older brother and partner, Stuart, who had built up resentment and frustration, and decided to unleash them on this particular morning, one week before the cafe's grand opening date.

Cafe Latte was an espresso bar located in Pocatello, Idaho, which opened in February 1998. Three siblings—Stuart Chan, Rob Chan, and Cynthia Chan—and a friend, Jeff Burns, formed a limited liability partnership and pooled their resources to build this business. Each partner had a 25 percent stake in the business. The partners had decided early in the summer of 1997 that an espresso bar was a business that could be quickly built with relatively low levels of capital, be quickly profitable, and could be maintained with minimal supervision if fully staffed.

Late in the summer of 1997, a space became available for lease at a very reasonable rate. The partnership had to make a decision—with the rent so low, they knew that they might lose the space if they didn't act quickly, so within 24 hours they decided they would take it if the lease was not longer than one year. Fortunately, the Chan siblings already knew this landlord from their parents' restaurant business. Since the Chan family was in good standing with him, he agreed to offer them a six-month lease with a discount for tenant improvements.

By early fall of 1997, construction had begun. The previous tenant had done no refurbishing, so the interior space was very old and dilapidated. Everything had to be torn down, ripped out, and replaced.

Cynthia had a friendly relationship with the contractor and the most free time out of the four partners. So they decided she would accompany the contractor to pick out the materials and the colors for the cafe. Cynthia had no idea what a monumental task she had been given. For a few hours every morning, she would meet with the contractor at a specified location, and he would take her through various restaurants and offices that he had previously remodeled. Together they would look at the different types of moldings, woods, and other fixtures and decide which she liked best.

Cynthia and the contractor would also meet at various espresso bars to decide which features Cynthia liked the most, and which ones were not very functional. After the initial plan of the cafe was sketched out, Cynthia had to make decisions about the color scheme of the furniture and the walls. This was a very important part of the design because the partners all wanted a "classy" feel and not a "thrift store" atmosphere.

During this phase of construction, Stuart supervised the construction work and acquired large pieces of machinery such as an ice maker, dishwasher, and deli case. Rob was not heavily involved during this phase, but he assisted Stuart in seeking the best pieces of machinery and later did much of the painting and clean-up after construction. Jeff was the only partner who lived in a different state. He was an engineer who resided full time in California, a silent partner due to geographical distance.

During this time, Cynthia also took two trips to the West Coast on behalf of the partnership. The first trip was to Seattle, Washington, where she enrolled in a course to learn the essentials of coffee and drink preparation. This course was vital to the business, since none of the partners had ever worked in an espresso bar. From this trip, Cynthia was able to create a menu and formulate a training program for future baristas (employees). The second trip was necessary in order to acquire the artwork that would decorate the walls of the espresso bar. The partners did not believe that the local print stores in Pocatello had much variety, so Cynthia was chosen to fly to San Francisco to find the appropriate pieces.

One week before the grand opening of the cafe, the contractor fell substantially behind, causing all partners to become concerned.

Cynthia Chan

Cynthia Chan had always been described as "old beyond her years" and an "independent spirit." She was born in 1969, the youngest of seven children. She had five elder brothers and one sister who was 13 years her senior. When Cynthia was eight years old, her parents opened a restaurant, which kept them away from home most of the day. Cynthia learned from that point on that she needed to be self-reliant, since her parents were not always available to take care of her.

In 1983, at age 14, Cynthia was in a terrible car accident and nearly lost her life. She was hospitalized for five weeks and underwent thirteen operations resulting from compound fractures of her right leg. As a result of this accident, Cynthia had a lot of social interaction with adults in the medical profession. She quickly learned that she needed to act like an adult if she wanted to be treated like one. Not only did she mature quickly, but she realized how life could be suddenly taken away. As a result, Cynthia learned that life was too short to be involved in petty arguments and that life was no fun without challenges.

Cynthia's adventurous spirit prompted her to get out of Idaho and see what else life had to offer. Right after graduation from high school, she headed to the West Coast. She stayed one year in Seattle, Washington, and then spent seven years in San Francisco, California. There she worked as a bank officer in a hectic, fast-paced branch of a large bank. When Cynthia tired of the "big city-corporate life" and the constant stress of dealing with other people's money, she headed back to Idaho in 1995 to try her hand at entrepreneurship.

Stuart Chan

Stuart was the middle child of the Chan family and was very bright and happy as a youngster. One odd aspect of Stuart's personality was his desire to excessively tease and taunt his younger siblings. It was almost a daily ritual that he would instigate some mean act against Rob or Cynthia.

As an adult, he majored in economics, graduating from the local university. He did well in his classes and had many friends. He was unable to pursue any kind of career in his field because his parents needed his help at their restaurant. He managed the 100-seat establishment, partly as an act of familial obligation, and partly because he wanted to be his "own boss." Later, Stuart began to feel resentment toward his parents and family because he felt trapped. Stuart had also stated once that he was mad at the family for not helping with the family business as much as he and that he was the one who was always "picking up the pieces" after the other siblings created "messes" within the business. He could not leave the business because his parents needed him; yet, he really had no work experience outside of the service industry and he had no desire to "break his back for someone else." He also resented Cynthia's lifestyle; she had traveled extensively and had a much more open schedule, which allowed her more freedom to explore her surroundings. As a result of this resentment, Stuart lashed out at Cynthia when he was angry with his family for feeling trapped. He felt like no one understood his fate, so in his rage, he would yell at anyone in the family who was nearby. Unfortunately, Cynthia was usually nearby since she was often defending her parents against Stuart's angry assaults. Oddly, Stuart's friends reported that he never got angry with them.

Rob Chan and Jeff Burns

Rob was situated on the family tree between Stuart and Cynthia. He was described as "happy-go-lucky" and an all-around nice guy who would give the shirt off his back if someone asked for it. He was never one to take charge of a project and was more a follower than a leader due to his fear of "stepping on someone's toes."

Jeff Burns became involved with the partnership due to his friendship with Stuart. They had been high school friends and had remained in contact with one another throughout the years. Stuart approached Jeff with the espresso bar idea, and Jeff thought that it was a good investment. He was approached mainly as a financial partner.

High Anxiety Before the Grand Opening

At the end of January 1998, one week before the grand opening of Cafe Latte, Cynthia walked into the kitchen of her parents' restaurant. She was slightly nervous, and at the same time, excited for the espresso bar to finally open. She had just returned from there and had practiced all the steps of drink preparation and cleanup.

As Cynthia prepared to make breakfast, she noticed Stuart muttering something under his breath. Cynthia asked him what was bothering him, and he angrily stated that she was not practicing enough on the drinks or learning how to use the espresso maker properly. Cynthia calmly replied that she did know how to make the drinks and reminded him that she was the one who went to Seattle for the initial training and then trained him (and the others) with her new knowledge. He angrily responded that she was not putting in as much time and effort as he was, and that she and Rob had been "slacking." He felt that Rob and Cynthia would not know how to train the employees when the time came.

Cynthia was outraged by these accusations. She did not believe that they should be wasting pounds and pounds of coffee on practice drinks and throwing them out—especially since they were not going to be the ones to actually tend the bar. By this time, Stuart's face was very red and he was obviously extremely angry. His last comments were a threat. He said that he was going to buy out Rob and Cynthia's stake of the partnership and run the business as he pleased. This was not the first time that he made this threat.

Cynthia was in shock; she could not believe that all her previous contributions were completely forgotten. She had assumed that each partner was doing his or her share of the tasks based on each one's specific talents, and that they were rapidly progressing toward a common goal. The worse part of the confrontation was that it took place in front of their parents and Rob, and with the employees overhearing.

Cynthia felt more frustrated than she had ever felt in her life. She knew that something had to change or their partnership was at stake. She stormed outside and looked up at the sky for answers. How should she handle this situation with just one week until the grand opening of Cafe Latte?

[Please do not read case B until instructed to do so by your instructor.]

Cafe Latte, LLC (B)

Cynthia was still stewing about the confrontation with Stuart and had not spoken to him in about 48 hours. During this time, Cynthia consulted with her other two partners and several of her friends whom she considered mentors. She weighed her options with them. The first option was to ignore Stuart's outbursts and dismiss them as part of his temper. The second option was to have Rob take over her share of the business and deal with Stuart. The third option was to take Stuart up on his offer to buy out her share.

Rob and Jeff did not know how to deal with the situation either. They knew that Stuart had a problem with anger, but they thought the best way to deal with him was just to let his temper fade—then he was usually fine. They did not fully realize the extent to which Cynthia had been the brunt of his angry episodes over the past three years, and that she was no longer able to deal with these flare-ups and maintain a good working relationship with him.

Rob and Cynthia talked about possibly having Rob take over Cynthia's share and make payments to her over time. This was not a feasible solution, since Rob did not have the financial capability, and Cynthia was not willing to be out of the picture if she still had a monetary stake in the venture.

Cynthia decided to take the third option. She thought she would surprise Stuart and take his threat seriously. She thought their differences were irreconcilable and she needed to remove herself from the situation. She believed that it was just a matter of time before Stuart had another angry episode. The only problem with this option was that Cynthia felt she had invested not only money into this venture but a lot of her time. She felt as if she was making a huge sacrifice for the benefit of the partnership and was not totally happy about it. The next day, Cynthia tallied up her financial contributions to the venture and handed it over to Stuart.

Stuart's Response

Stuart looked at the sheet of expenses that Cynthia handed him and left it on the table. Two days later, Stuart left a three-page handwritten apology in Cynthia's car. Not only did he apologize for his temper, but he also outlined all the reasons that he believed Cynthia should stay with the venture, and how her skills were invaluable to the company. Stuart and Rob knew that the initial six to twelve months would be important to the success of the cafe, which would require 150 percent input from all the partners at this crucial time. Stuart knew that he could not lose Cynthia now, since she and Rob were going to be the main principals getting this venture off the ground.

Cynthia's Final Act

Cynthia was surprised by the apology letter but felt it was merely a "bandage" over the larger problem. She realized that she could not force Stuart to buy her share, so she decided to work with Rob and try to arrange a better working schedule so she would not have to interact so often with Stuart.

The revised schedule was the best solution that Rob, Cynthia, and Jeff could come up with. After the opening of the espresso bar, the partners decided that Rob would be the on-site manager running the operation, with Cynthia and Stuart assisting.

Changing Quotas

by Susan Steele

Susan Steele, a seasoned sales representative, knew there was a potential sale looming. Her customer, Tom Leney, senior vice president at Fidelity Federal Bank, wanted to change the bank's image and considered updated ATMs as a good vehicle to initiate the change. Susan saw this as an opportunity to sell a large number of ATMs; however, it was a long way from being a real deal. She needed to clarify the customer's needs and enlist the help of her new and old managers to prepare a sales presentation for the executives in her organization, as well as Fidelity Federal Bank. Susan was determined to achieve a win-win situation for all parties.

The two main parties involved in the transaction were Fidelity Federal Bank and Susan's company, Diebold. Fidelity was a financial institution with more than $4 billion in assets. Fidelity was under the direction of Albert Greenwood, CEO, a visionary who wanted to make his bank different from others by jumping on the technology bandwagon first. Diebold, in business since 1859, created vaults and equipment for the financial industry. Diebold was a cash-rich company that generated over $1 billion in sales annually, much from the ATM market. Susan's goal was to bring these two parties together to make a deal.

Key Players

The key players in the incident were Carroll Lawerence, Susan's former boss, who now held a different position at her office. Carroll was an old, wily Texan, who would use his good ol' boy accent to make himself sound down-to-earth and maybe not so smart, but those who underestimated him received a rude awakening. Carroll previously worked for IBM in sales for 10 years prior to joining Diebold. By the time he became a sales manager, there wasn't a lot you could tell him about people or how to make a sale. His best attribute in a sales cycle was his creativity. When Carroll put deals together, he thought out of the box, or unconventionally, to stimulate the sales process.

Another key player was Tom Leney, the senior vice president at Fidelity. Tom was quiet, open-minded, and ready to listen to ideas that would help him achieve the bank's objectives. He had a dry sense of humor that surfaced when he felt relaxed around a person. When he was not relaxed, he was very direct, which seemed to make him easier to work with as he didn't need to be second-guessed.

Ron Tenuta, divisional vice president, was another key player. He was not a people person and did not come from a sales background. He was very numbers oriented and not predisposed to favor a creative, out-of-the-box deal. The pressure from his extensive responsibilities could have enhanced his somewhat distant way of dealing with people.

Ron Tenuta hired Bob Ricucci, regional sales manager. Bob was young and lacked sales experience, which became apparent when he tried to creatively come up with a deal where no deal initially existed. Bob meant well most of the time; however, his ego and lack of real knowledge sometimes made him a frustrating source and difficult to rely on. Bob was responsible for nine sales representatives and a sales quota of $22 million.

Susan Steele

The last key player, Susan Steele, was a senior sales representative. Susan's territory mainly consisted of southern California financial institutions with assets of $4 billion and under. She was perceived as a successful sales representative; she met her yearly sales quotas, was able to generate new business, and enjoyed her work. She felt frustrated at times working for a large company, as the internal politics could be difficult. When Susan was first hired at Diebold, it was a male-dominated company. Out of 700 sales representatives, 10 were women. After three years with the company, she had seen Diebold expand its sales force and recruit several female sales representatives.

Susan had been working hard for a reputation as a sales representative who could produce even in the most challenging markets, Los Angeles being one of them. In Susan's first year as a representative she exceeded her quota by 127 percent in 9 months versus 12. After this, the company took away all of her larger accounts that had assets in excess of $4 billion. The company explained that as a regional representative she would only have accounts with assets under $4 billion in the future. After the change in her territory, a decision was made not to raise Susan's quota, for she now had fewer accounts with less purchasing power. Despite the changes, Susan had another great selling year and was able to surpass her quota by 377 percent. Susan had won numerous awards for sales over the last three years and was satisfied with her performance. She wanted to move into a management position, at some point, but felt the company would not take her seriously, despite her success.

Potential for a BIG Deal

The potential to make a big sale surfaced during a customer golf outing. Susan and her boss, Bob, had just finished a game of golf with Tom Leney and one of the other senior vice presidents from the bank. Susan did not have the opportunity to take these customers out golfing previously, so she was anxious that the day would go well. Her boss had opted out of lunch, which bothered her, as she thought this was the best time to bond with the customer. So be it. She resolved to go out to lunch without him. She kept the customers interested with stimulating conversation and just the right amount of probing questions to determine if there was any business to be had in the account. They were all trying to get comfortable with each other. Tom Leney, the vice president in charge of retail banking, settled in his chair and checked out the surrounding club atmosphere. As is common in many business functions, an awkward silence arose when the players began to size each other up. Everyone went through the same mantra—"think before you speak and don't give information away."

Lunch had been ordered, and everyone was at that comfortable point where they laughed about their golf game, chit-chatted about their families, and discussed everything else but work. Oddly, the reason they were all together had eluded them as a topic thus far. Susan didn't want to be the one to break the amicable spell but considering that she had just spent $300 of the company's money on golf and lunch, she felt obligated. She crept up on the subject of business like a swimmer creeps up to a pool of very cold water, testing the water timidly before deciding to wade in. Her approach seemed to work as Tom and the other vice president, Bob Grider, began to tell her all sorts of interesting things. Tom surprised her when he said that the bank would be interested in potentially changing all of its rather new ATMs for an even newer model with more high-tech features. Questions flooded her mind: Why would they want to make such a huge capital outlay? Would they really want to change machines that still had to be on their books for a considerable amount of money? What was the driving motivation for this move and how could she get them to consider it more seriously?

She was anxious to question them, but her sales instinct said, " Take your time and don't barrage them with too much at once." Tentatively, she asked if they were serious, and if she put together a deal that could give them new machines without financially impacting them too heavily, would they take a look at it? They both acknowledged that the potential for a deal was real, but it would have to be a good proposal. After leaving the golf course, Susan casually calculated the numbers as she drove back home and realized a deal of that size could generate $2 million in sales. This would help her exceed her quota and generate a great commission. She just had to figure out how she could make it happen.

Thinking Out of the Box

As she neared home she anxiously phoned her manager to tell him the great news she uncovered at the golf lunch, the promise of a large prospect. Her manager's response was less than enthusiastic. Maybe the deal sounded too far out, or maybe he was busy. However, from that point on, she referred to her old manager for help in creating the deal. Susan didn't want to have to sell the manager on a scheme before selling the customer. She felt her manager should have been excited from the get-go.

As the week progressed, she worked with her old manager Carroll Lawerence. They brainstormed, role played, and thought out all of the options. Susan felt comfortable with her old boss because he never criticized any of the ideas she put forth. Susan and Carroll sat in a quiet office with a note pad. They felt it was imperative not to have any interruptions while they were trying to think strategically. First, Carroll would blurt out an idea, then Susan would add to it. This approach went on for hours until Susan said, "By golly, this looks like a damn good business deal. It is financially sound, it achieves the customer's objectives, and is easy to understand." Essentially, the deal was worked from the premise that if Diebold could write off the balance of the current machines, this would free them up financially and enable them to invest in new technology. The deal was similar to what could be done if you had an old car and wanted to get a new one. If you did not have enough cash up front to purchase the new one, the car dealer may buy your current car for blue book price and finance the rest, allowing you to get a new car for little or no cash outlay. Susan felt confident that Fidelity's customers would be willing to pay something for the newer technology as long as they could get the old machines to appear as though they never existed on their books.

She phoned Fidelity and learned that the machines were on their books for $700,000. Susan had to figure out a way to make that amount go away. This was her chance at a $2 million deal, and it was worth the mental gymnastics.

For the next two weeks, she refined and checked on terms. Finally, she had a deal to present to the customer. However, before selling the deal to the customer, she now had to convince her own company to support the terms. First, Susan planned to offer to buy back the customer's old ATM machines. She would have Diebold write out a check for the 37 units the customer currently had installed, at a rate of $9,000 a unit, for a total of $333,000. Second, once Fidelity signed the purchase order, had all the new units installed, and paid for them in full, Diebold would write the bank a refund check for $396,048. In total, Fidelity would receive a refund in the amount of $729,048. To get the money for the second check, she merely sold the equipment to the customer at a 20 percent discount. Once the order was entered, she had it internally restructured on Diebold's books for a 38 percent discount; this gave her the money she needed to give back to the customer. As simple as this seemed, it was easier said than done.

Many large companies, such as Diebold that do over $1 billion a year in sales, have a lot of bureaucracy. Susan felt the bureaucracy in her company bred complacency and made people less apt to think out of the box.

Susan's real sales cycle began when she worked to sell her manager on her sales concept. Fortunately, her manager saw dollar signs, and said he would back her up as she moved the deal up the corporate flagpole. The next level was Ron Tenuta, the divisional vice president. Susan pictured Ron as a great mannequin because his expressions rarely changed, and his movements remained stiff, like he was made of cardboard. Ron's background was service, not sales, so he usually suffered in silence when he heard deals that were out of the box. As Ron listened to her pitch during the first go-round, he didn't get it, so he asked her to put it in writing, which she did, and they had a second go-round. Once the second go-round was over, Susan had him convinced it could work. Finally, she sent the proposal to the president of North American Sales.

After the deal went around the company and received everyone's blessing, Susan was able to present it to the customer. Susan outlined the proposal on one page to enable Fidelity to visualize the whole picture at once, while keeping it simple enough to understand. She faxed the proposal to Tom and prepared to wait for his response.

After a couple of days, she phoned Tom and asked what he thought of the deal. At first, he was a bit confused by how it was written out, but after Susan went over the details, he responded quite enthusiastically. Susan was elated, as she felt she was on the right track. They discussed some other terms that Fidelity wanted, and confirmed that he would take it to the CEO to get some feedback. Things were rolling in the right direction when, all of a sudden, a roadblock popped up in front of Susan.

Questioning Susan's Quota

As her deal began to look like a reality, more and more people seemed to get interested in it. Ron Tenuta, the vice president, began to question her current quota. He explained that she had already made her numbers for the year and that this sale would afford her to far exceed her numbers. Susan couldn't understand what the problem was and wondered why he wouldn't want her to far exceed her numbers. After a heated discussion between her manager, the vice president, and Susan, it was decided that her quota would have to be raised. Susan was taken by surprise because they usually didn't raise quotas six months into the year. They said she could wait and see if she got the order before they raised it, in which case they would raise it from $1.2 million to $3.0 million, or she could let them raise it now to $2 million and, perhaps, not get the deal but have a higher quota for the rest of the year. Susan decided she would let them raise her quota to $2 million now rather than endure the "wait and see" approach, which would raise her quota to $3 million.

Susan thought about why her quota may have been raised. First, the company may have perceived that Susan would make too much money if her quota was not raised and this could cause problems with the other sales reps. Second, the company may have also perceived that Susan didn't have to work very hard for such a large sale and determined that she did not deserve such a large compensation, as the deal came together so quickly. Finally, the company may have decided that Susan had a good year the previous year and wanted to challenge her. They may have regretted not raising her quota in the beginning of the year and rationalized that they needed to amend their error.

Susan had already made her quota for the year, which was $1.2 million. At Diebold, once a salesperson reached his or her quota level, he or she was entitled to additional percentage points. These points kicked in once the numbers were achieved and allowed a salesperson to make double or triple the amount of commission. To date, Susan had met and exceeded her current quota of $1.2 million and was owed close to $50,000 in commission. The new commission structure affected everything she had sold, for it would be recalculated at the new quota structure. She would initially lose $40,000 of commission because all of the extra percentage points would be taken away from orders she had already received. So she needed the Fidelity deal not only to get ahead but also to recoup money she had already earned, and to keep pace with her newly acquired quota.

Susan's manager approached her, for he wanted to know if the deal was really going to happen. When a rep has a $2 million deal in the works, a lot people become interested in the outcome. The good news was that Fidelity was leaning her way, and the deal was getting the thumbs up from the CEO and president of the bank. She did have an inside track on how this customer may react because last year she sold them some high-tech machines and they really liked them. She knew that these units would fit well into the bank's marketing plan and felt confident the deal would come together.

As she waited for another two weeks, Susan busied herself doing proposals and taking other customers to the Diebold showroom in San Francisco. One afternoon, while sitting in the Oakland airport, she received Fidelity's response to her proposal. As she was sitting in the airport, she checked her voice mail. The usual messages droned by and then she heard Tom's voice. He said, "Susan, if you are not sitting down you might want to." Her stomach dropped because she thought he was going to say they decided against the deal, but he went on, "We have decided to do the deal. Bring the paperwork by next week and we will get it signed. Thank you and congratulations." She could not contain her happiness. She felt as though she had climbed Mount Everest and circumnavigated the globe all at once. Her sense of achievement was great. It is interesting to note that the thought of good commissions was the last thing to enter her mind. Susan's main feeling was a sense of great accomplishment.

Computer Services Team at AVIONICS

by Teri C. Tompkins, Pepperdine University

John Johnson, a top executive at AVIONICS who was partially responsible for information systems, was contemplating a government contract directive that called for an integration of the computer information systems into a "service center" concept. He was also aware that management had issued a directive to cut costs, and that he had not been inspired by the service center manager's performance for some time. He wondered if the service contract idea was an opportunity to address all three issues at once.

John was known for his ability to empower people. He was dedicated to continual process improvement techniques, and he had put together a number of process improvement teams, focusing on concurrent engineering and total quality management (TQM). He prided himself on his ability to help teams improve quality and process. People respected John's abilities, and he had moved up rapidly in the organization. His excellent interpersonal skills made him well liked and influential at AVIONICS.

In John's readings of total quality management and process improvement, he had been impressed with the concept of a "leaderless team" or "autonomous work groups." He wondered if the service center concept could be an opportunity to experiment with the idea. After some thought, he decided to lay off the computer information systems supervisor and create a leaderless team. He changed the name from "computer information systems" to "computer service center," and let team members know that their purpose was to integrate their systems to provide quality service to the customers.

As John expected, the laid-off supervisor, Glen Smith, was not happy and immediately filed a grievance, requesting reinstatement. He was allowed to stay as a member of the team until a decision could be made about his status. Even with the grievance, John felt satisfied that he had solved some of his problems. Glen wouldn't be a problem now that he was just a member.

John decided to start the team off right with a two-day, intensive training session. At the training session, he told the team members he was empowering them to change their own destiny. "You have the opportunity to control your own work," John enthusiastically told them. "No one is a leader—*you* are all responsible. That means if you have a problem, don't come running to me—you are in charge!"

Using large sheets of newsprint, the group listed their goals and expectations. They decided they wanted to achieve a collective identity. John instructed them on breakthrough analysis and told them about leaderless teams. Team members were impressed by John's knowledge of the subject. William Ashby, a MacIntosh specialist, listened with interest. He really liked what John was saying about total quality management. He had read a few books on the subject and, listening to John, he felt inspired about really doing it.

The First Meeting

Shortly after the off-site training session, team members gathered for their first meeting. Eight people sat at a large rectangular table. William, the MacIntosh specialist, looked around the room. He had more or less worked with several of these people in the past; at least they had shared the same large office space. There was Alyne, the VAX systems administrator, and her assistant, Frank. William recognized Russ, the IBM PC specialist and his counterpart. Glen, their former supervisor, was there, trying to blend in. Three other people he didn't know very well were also present: Rachel, the database support specialist, Herald, from business operations, and the assistant business manager, Carol.

A few people chatted with each other. Carol appeared engrossed in a memo. Glen sat with his arms folded, leaning back in his chair. William wondered who was going to get the meeting started. People were looking uncomfortable, waiting and wondering what would happen next. "Maybe I should say something," William thought to himself. He cleared his throat.

"Well, here we all are," he said. William hesitated, to see if anyone else wanted to take the lead. Everyone except Carol, who still seemed engrossed in her memo, stared at him. "I guess we should get started," William announced, hoping someone would offer a suggestion. He waited again. Again, everyone stared at him.

"Well, I for one was really excited about what John had to say at our off-site training." William looked around the room; a few people's heads nodded. "So I guess we should get started," William repeated, feeling a bit foolish.

Glen, the former supervisor, sat watching the group. "Oh, brother!" he thought. "This is going to be a problem, a real problem." He watched William struggle to lead the group.

William continued: "John suggested that we elect a leader from among ourselves to act as a volunteer leader of sorts. Does anyone have any suggestions?"

"Yeah, let's hurry this up," said Russ, the IBM PC specialist. "I've got 10 people who need to be hard-wired, breathing down my neck." Russ continued, "I nominate you, William. You seem interested, and I really don't care who our leader is."

Some of the people looked at Russ with embarrassment. They had lots of work to do, too, but wouldn't have put it so bluntly. "He sure is a pain," thought Alyne. She turned to William and smiled. "Yes, I think William would be good. Would you be interested, William?" she asked.

"Well, I guess I would. I've never played on a formal team before, and I don't know what to do, but I'm willing to give it a shot." William felt the blood rising up to his ears. "I guess, unless there are any objections, I'll volunteer to be leader." Since no one said anything, William became the leader.

The group spent the next 20 minutes trying to figure out what it was supposed to be doing. They weren't sure what a TQM team was, or what it meant to integrate their various jobs to "create a service team." Most of the people sat and listened while William, Alyne, and Rachel talked. Russ stated again that he really needed to get back to work. The group decided to continue the discussion during the next meeting, a week away.

The Volunteer Leader Prepares

William told his wife that night about his election as leader of the group. "I'm not sure what to do. Maybe I'll check out the bookstore, and see if I can find some books on the subject." William drove to the bookstore and searched through the business section. He found several books on TQM that looked promising, plus one called *How to Make Prize Winning Teams*, which he thought was a real find.

That night, he began reading *How to Make Prize Winning Teams*. He was inspired by what he read, and he thought it was "doable" for his team.

The next week, the team gathered once more around the rectangular table. Russ, the IBM specialist, was absent because of "pressing business," but everyone else was present. William started things off by telling them about the books. He suggested that everyone should get a copy and read it.

"I think we need to begin figuring out how to improve our work," William told them. He proceeded to tell them about how they should look at each of their areas, and look for ways to improve it. William looked down at the notes he had taken from the book. He wanted to make sure he told them all exactly how it should be done; he didn't want to get it wrong.

Alyne interrupted him. She didn't like the way William seemed to be telling them what to do. "I think before we go charging down that street, we need to decide how we are going to decide things. I, for one, don't want people telling me what to do about my area." A few people nodded. "I think everyone should have a vote in these changes."

"Yes, I agree," said Frank, her assistant. "Majority rules; no one should have more say-so than anyone else."

"Fine," said William, but he couldn't help feeling that something had just gone wrong. The team agreed to vote on all matters. People started fidgeting in their seats, so William suggested that they end the meeting. "Everyone should try to buy the books and read them before our next meeting," he said.

During the next few months, William tried in vain to get the group to read the books. He thought if they would read them, they'd understand what he'd been talking about.

He felt pretty disheartened as he spoke to his wife that night. "Everyone wants to just go along," he told her. "We've got all these individuals on the team, and they only seem to care about their own turf. I thought we were starting to make progress last week when a few people started talking about the common complaint their customers had about reaching them, but then it became a discussion about why their customers didn't understand. I've learned you can't dictate to them. I have to win them over, but I don't know how. I'm going for a drive to think this out."

As William drove toward the beach, he thought about his job. He wasn't having much fun. Every meeting was the same thing. Members had to vote on every little thing that was brought up. If someone in the group didn't want to do it, that person just didn't vote. Or the person would go along with everyone else and vote but not follow through. He saw no evidence that anyone wanted to make it work. He wished he could go to his supervisor, John, but John had maintained a strict hands-off approach with the team since the in-service training. He felt that John had cut them loose, to sink or swim. They were definitely sinking.

"Maybe there is too much diversity on this team," he thought. "I need training on how to bring a diverse group together." He decided to see if he could get some training to help him out of the hole he'd crawled into.

William Voted Out

When William approached the human resources department about the training, he was told that his group did not have the budget for that kind of training. William angrily left the office, feeling very discouraged.

Over the next two months, it became painfully obvious that the group wasn't working. Some team members argued constantly, and some avoided conflict at all cost. Carol, the assistant business manager, requested a stress leave. She felt she couldn't take the problems and responsibility any longer. No one could agree on the team's goals, or how they were going to integrate their "service team." They felt frustrated with John, their manager, and thought he was unpredictable. John had a reputation for being a supportive and creative manager, yet with this team he was distant. They wondered why he didn't act like the manager others said he was.

Finally, at one meeting six months after the team began, Alyne, the VAX specialist, spoke up, "Look, William, this isn't working. We need a new leader." Everyone else agreed and, after some discussion, they voted in Glen, their former supervisor, as their "volunteer" leader. Glen, who had recently won his grievance against the layoff, was ready for the assignment.

William felt hurt. "That's it, I give up," he thought. "From now on, I'm looking out for my own group. I've been neglecting the Mac users, but no more."

About the time that Glen became "volunteer" leader, John was transferred to another assignment, and Barbara, the director of business management, became the group's manager. She told team members they needed to get better at serving their customers.

Glen, who had more leadership skills than William, recognized that the team was at a crisis point. He decided to try to build trust among the team members by working on continuous process improvement (CPI). He thought they might be able to pull it off if they just had enough time.

After four months, Barbara, the team manager, pulled the plug and ordered the team to go back to the structure it had nearly a year ago. A few people, and particularly Glen, were disappointed. "I was just beginning to feel like we were going to make it. The other team members were right—the company doesn't support teams. They just give a lot of lip service, but there is no management commitment."

The team went back to its old structure. John, their former manager, looked back at what happened. "They are still having problems serving their customers. I ran a bizarre experiment by cutting them loose. I took away all their support systems, and told them they were all equal people. It was a big mistake."

NOTE: For a background on AVIONICS, see Appendix A of <u>Cost and Schedule Team at AVIONICS</u>.

Cost and Schedule Team at AVIONICS

by Teri C. Tompkins, Pepperdine University

Crisis Management

In early 1993, members of the cost and schedule team were frustrated. For more than two and a half months, they had been trying to do their job with too few resources. They were short of people and computers. As part of the defense contract that the team was working on, the government had mandated that the cost and scheduling functions, which were traditionally two separate units, be completely integrated. Learning how to integrate their functions with so few resources and support seemed impossible. In addition, they were led by a "working" supervisor, Dan, who was often too busy doing his own work to help the team sort through its problems.

Things were coming to a head. Alice, a cost specialist and one of seven members of the team, had just had a loud argument with one of the scheduling specialists, Jim. The argument had occurred right in the middle of the third-floor hallway, where he and a few of the other team members were located. The deadline for submitting a report to the government was two days away, and Alice had just found yet another error from whom she described as "her inept counterpart."

Janie, a scheduling specialist, could hear the argument through her partition. She called a teammate, Scott: "I'm going crazy. We've got to do something about this constant bickering and ego-tripping."

"What would you suggest?"

"First, I think we should go see John." After discussing their problem with John Johnson, Dan's supervisor, they made a decision to call a team meeting, without Dan, and clear the air.

The First Meeting

A few days later, the team met outside by the lunch area far enough away from other employees not to be overheard. John Johnson passed out three-by-five cards and asked each person to write down his or her concerns anonymously. The list was extensive, but the major complaints were:

1. Our biggest problem is team communication.
2. We lack the people and hardware resources to get things done.
3. Our supervisor, Dan, lacks the knowledge to understand our problems and lacks the political savvy to help us when push comes to shove. He is so busy with his own projects that he doesn't have time to support this team. In addition, he constantly yells and screams at us.
4. We're operating out of "crisis" management.
5. We're stabbing each other in the back.

After John read the cards out loud, Janie related her perception of the problem. "We all want to do our jobs well. We're professionals, and we care about the quality of our work. But the truth is, we aren't doing a very good job meeting our goals. We're supposed to be working together to meet our goals. Instead, we're fighting among ourselves, missing deadlines, and blaming each other."

Several members of the team nodded their heads in agreement. Alice spoke up. "I'm relieved to hear you say what I've been thinking." Scott nodded and looked around at the group. "Yes, somehow our meeting together like this gives me hope that we might be able to work our way out of this mess."

Janie picked up her pad of paper. "Let's list what we need to accomplish our job." After an hour and a half of furious writing and brainstorming, the team members seemed satisfied with their analysis.

In addition to recognizing that they needed to "help each other rather than harp on each other," team members had the following list of concerns, which they thought only management could deal with:

1. We need to be located close together so we can communicate better.
2. Our supervisor, Dan, doesn't know how to manage, and he's of no use in helping us solve our day-to-day problems because he's so busy doing his own work. In addition, he is overly critical and controlling.

3. Our work is dependent on the use of a MacIntosh; yet due to reduced budgets, half of us still have IBM PCs. We need more MacIntoshes.

4. The software program that we are supposed to use to write our integrated reports doesn't have any documentation, and we don't know how to use it. We need training for every member of the team.

5. Our project plan calls for us to have 12 people on our team. We have seven and we're all working about 70 hours a week, including weekends, just to keep up.

6. We need to be more informed. We feel like lackeys rather than active participants in solving our problems.

John agreed to work on the list and suggested the team meet again, without Dan, to continue discussions.

Management's Response

Over the course of the week, the cost and schedule team members were happy that John seemed to take their concerns seriously. In fact, he acted on one of their suggestions immediately by creating space for the team on the second floor. He seemed sympathetic to the team's workload, and said he would get some new members transferred to the team soon. He also agreed to try to share more information with them on a timely basis.

Team members were unhappy with John's response to their other concerns. He seemed unwilling to respond to their complaints about Dan, and preferred the "wait and see" approach. Their plea for MacIntosh computers on every desk was denied because of "other projects with higher priority, needing MacIntoshes more." John explained that the switch to MacIntosh computers was very expensive, and that "tight budgets and poor business outlook" had slowed the acquisition of additional hardware. With its high overhead, he said, management couldn't afford additional outside software training for team members.

The Second Meeting

At the next meeting with John, members of the cost and schedule team agreed that they should meet every Wednesday to discuss their issues. After discussing management's response to their requests, they came up with a plan to deal with their supervisor.

"Dan's stupid mandates are driving me crazy. I find myself not wanting to do anything that he tells me I *have* to do," Jim complained.

Alice nodded. "He's so critical. Last week, Dan yelled at me for missing a deadline after I worked 75 hours to accomplish the impossible. Why should I work my butt off if that's all the thanks I'm going to get!"

Ken looked thoughtful. "I agree he is difficult to work with, but I think we should try to put ourselves in his shoes. Besides the fact that he has lousy management skills, he's also very busy. If we show him how our meeting together, and taking over some of his duties, will relieve him of pressure, then perhaps he will be more willing to give us the freedom to do our jobs."

"Yes, management is always talking about *empowerment*, and that is exactly what we're requesting." Janie pressed her hands together. "We want to build our team spirit and increase our skills and achievement."

"I agree," Scott looked serious, "but I'd like to broach another subject. I'm concerned about how our group works together. We are constantly at each other's throats. We're so overworked and under so much pressure that we stress out. Sometimes I just need someone to help me out of my jam, but I know each of you is busy, too. Sometimes I get so angry at what I perceive as lack of support."

"I feel the same frustration," Alice looked up at the sky. "I guess we've all been feeling this way. It's not so much that we don't care about each other, it's just that each of us has different ways of coping with our stress. I think we need to agree to set our differences aside and try to like each other."

After more discussion about team communications, teammates agreed to fight among themselves more fairly and with more concern for each other. They also agreed to invite Dan to participate in the team meetings. The meeting was adjourned with almost everyone feeling better about the team dynamics.

Data Loss!

The next Thursday afternoon, Kim was transferring data from the DOS program to the MAC program. She and a teammate, Ralph, had spent the whole week gathering data and inputting it into the correct report format for the weekly report to their military client.

"Oh, no!" exclaimed Kim. "NO, NO, NO!"

Janie came into Kim's cubicle. Kim was staring at the computer screen with a despairing look. Kim looked up at her, "It's lost. I hit the wrong key and it's lost! I hate this damn program!"

"What's lost?"

"All the work we did this week."

"Don't you have a backup?"

"No, I was in such a hurry to get this transferred so that we could edit the report in time to make our deadline that I didn't make a copy. Damn!" Kim looked distraught.

"All right, don't panic, maybe we can retrieve it."

Over the next several hours, various members of the team tried to retrieve the lost data. Ralph looked up. "It's no use. I guess Kim and I will have to work around the clock and get it done."

Scott pulled up a chair. "You still won't make the deadline. I'll stay and help."

"So will I," Janie offered.

Soon most of the team members had offered their help. By four in the morning, they had re-created the data and input it into the system. Although they were tired, they felt good that they had worked together to meet their goals.

The Learning Begins

The government contract report required use of a software program called Integration of Job Measurement and Planning Program, or IJMPP for short, which integrated the cost and scheduling functional reports. The team had resisted using the program. Partly in response to Kim's accidental data erasure and partly because of the contract requirements, Janie and Scott decided that they must learn to use the new software program. Another engineer at their company had designed the program, but, unfortunately, there was no documentation, and few people knew how to use it.

After much frustration and experimentation, Janie and Scott became fairly proficient at using the program. It was just what the team needed to reduce the amount of time spent on its reports. Soon other members of the team were asking Janie and Scott to integrate their own data files using IJMPP. Unfortunately, this added an extra burden on Janie and Scott. After a few weeks of overwork, they brought it to the team's attention at a Wednesday meeting.

Kim nodded after Janie and Scott expressed their concern. "You're right. It's not fair that just because you took the initiative to learn the program that the rest of us should ask you to do our work. We're a team, but this is asking too much."

"I really resist learning this program, but I guess we really need it to get our job done," Freda said.

Everyone agreed that this was the next logical step to accomplishing the team's goals, and that it was the only fair thing to do for Janie and Scott.

Jim jumped in. "It sounds like it would be better if we all learned the program." He turned to Janie and Scott. "Would you be willing to teach us?"

Janie and Scott pushed aside much of their regular work for the next two weeks to teach the program to the team. Even after lessons, members called on Janie or Scott when they had software problems. However, after a time, most team members became proficient enough to solve most of their own problems. Although Janie and Scott still tended to be the resident experts, their teammates had learned the program well enough to use it without constantly depending on Janie or Scott to rescue them. Over time, members turned to each other rather than to Janie or Scott; if the problem did not require expert knowledge, they would simply ask the team member whose office was located nearby.

Collective Learning

Members of the cost and schedule team noticed that although they were still busy, the work seemed more fun. They attributed this to the fact that members seemed more supportive. They were learning how to get around the various members' moods, and to use the strengths and weaknesses of the members' work styles. For example, it was well known that when Alice was under stress, she became argumentative and illogical. However, members now knew that she was also extremely dedicated and rarely made mistakes. They could count on her to find quickly the error they had spent all morning searching for in their data.

Jim, on the other hand, was very sloppy in his work. He just didn't seem to have the commitment to professionalism that most of the team had. But at their monthly pizza party, Jim was really fun. He had a great sense of humor and was usually the last to leave the party. Jim added a sense of comic relief when the going got rough.

Janie was the team's informal leader. She always seemed able to clarify the issues, and she helped the team recognize problems in meeting its objectives. She was always available to coach another team member. She once spent the whole day teaching Kim to use one of their programs. But she did not know when to say "No." Sometimes she worked far into the night or on weekends to catch up.

Team members were just beginning to size up Sharon, one of four new members added since they complained to management. Her presence on the team was valued because of her technical knowledge of the data system. Her knowledge made it possible to have one less member on the team. However, team members were concerned that Sharon, who needed to use a MacIntosh, did not have one; she borrowed time on teammates' computers. After several weeks of this, the team decided that Jim would give Sharon his MacIntosh, and Sharon would give Jim her IBM. Jim would feed information to Kim via DOS. Kim, who worked most closely with Jim and frequently had to correct his sloppy work, thought this arrangement wouldn't be a problem because she needed to double-check his work anyway. Everyone, including Jim, seemed satisfied with the arrangement.

Six and a Half Months After the Team Began

Several other norms were emerging during the team's Wednesday meetings and during informal gatherings in the hall and cubicles. First, members were finding it increasingly easier to express their concerns to teammates. If a member was falling behind schedule, he or she admitted it to the rest of the team rather than trying to cover up. Mistakes were discussed much more openly. The attitude was, "Mistakes happen, so what are we going to do about it?"

Second, during meetings, either Janie or Scott would probe for details. The resulting increase in detailed reporting made it easier for team members to know where they were in accomplishing their weekly goals. In addition, as problems and successes were revealed in more detail, team members could learn vicariously.

"We looked at why we missed our deadlines, like not getting the word out on time, or how we can get product managers to get data to us, so we could do our job," Janie explained.

Third, members became much more willing to share information with each other. They worked hard at passing along any bit of news as soon as it was heard. For example, if Ken heard from someone in the lunch line that the company might be buying more MacIntoshes, he would quickly tell another member. That member would tell another, and so on. The sharing of information helped members feel that they were "in the loop."

Fourth, the team was taking on more of the group's management functions. Usually, someone would suggest how to break down the tasks and make sure that the parts were assigned to individuals. Rather than depend on management to provide learning opportunities, members formed mentor relationships with each other to increase their learning. Members of the team were still hesitant to tap their supervisor Dan's knowledge because they thought he was overly critical. However, Dan now participated regularly in the Wednesday meetings. Members of the group tolerated him at work and liked him at the pizza parties, but they didn't trust him. He expressed a desire to be open to change, but when push came to shove, they knew that he would lambaste a member in front of everyone. In addition, they still found him lacking at passing on critical information.

In exchange for being so open, members expected increased loyalty. Talking behind each other's back was considered in poor taste. Complaining outside the group was considered treason. Members began to think that they were making an investment in each other, not the team or the company.

Making and Improving Forecasts

Members spent much of their meeting time attempting to improve their ability to accomplish their tasks. For example, they found that it invariably took twice as long to do a task as they predicted, so they developed a formula for estimating completion time. They found that the "rules of thumb" provided a baseline from which they could measure their progress. Each week, they would attempt to improve their predictions by learning from experience. They also learned to expect certain patterns of peak pressure they described as a "rolling wave."

Janie explains: "The crest of the wave is a major crisis crunch. Not only do we have to do our normal work, but we also have to do contract planning. Fortunately, this is the third time we've done planning, so we're better at it. We're sharing how to do things. It's no longer the individual trying to make himself or herself look better by learning something, and not sharing it with the rest of us. Now we hurry up and share our ideas."

Success Feels Good!

About nine months after the cost and schedule team began as a team, the government audited its work. Audits usually were grueling, five-day experiences in which every inch of data was scrutinized for discrepancies or problems. Surprisingly, three and a half days into the audit, government auditors finished. The auditors couldn't say enough good things about the team. They were impressed with the quality and consistency of the team's data and management processes. News of this excellent report spread throughout the company. The cost and schedule team was held up as an example of what a good team could do.

Each member of the cost and schedule team gave full credit to the total team. "Superstar" members, like Janie and Scott, praised the team for its efforts. "Without working together, we could never have accomplished this," stated Janie.

"Pressure is okay if success and praise go with it," commented Scott.

"Yes, success makes it better," smiled Alice.

"We learn from the negative, but we need the positive to keep going," said Sharon.

"I needed feedback to know how we were doing. I wasn't convinced this was working, but seeing it work has convinced me," exclaimed Jim.

Appendix A – Background of AVIONICS

Avionics was a subsidiary of a large North American–based corporation named National Corporation Alliance (NCA). NCA was a market leader in a number of businesses including financial markets, real estate, and the defense industry. The defense industry units of NCA were not market leaders, but were successful as a subcontractor for the leading defense industry corporations. The headquarters of the defense industry division was located in Los Angeles County in southern California.

The defense industry units of NCA had several divisions. One of the most successful had been the electronics division. The electronics division's primary focus was in the area of electronic-sensing devices, such as specialized antennas and other receivers using digital and analog technologies. AVIONICS was one of three subsidiaries in the electronics division. It was located in San Diego County in southern California. The second subsidiary, bought by NCA in the mid-1980s, was located in Silicon Valley, California. A small electronic manufacturing subsidiary, located in Colorado, was also purchased around that time.

AVIONICS was founded as a spin-off from the Los Angeles–based division when executives decided that electronic sensing was an important area that needed specialized focus. Elite engineers and top scientists were chosen to start the new venture. In the mid-1970s, property was purchased in northern San Diego County where the weather was known to be mild and the schools excellent. They built a beautiful facility, and engineers, technicians, and scientists clamored for positions.

AVIONICS did not manufacture products. Its focus was on research and development of electronic systems. The government would specify a certain type of electronic-sensing system that it needed, such as one that could hear over certain distances or distinguish voices from white noise. The engineers and scientists would then seek ways to design the product. They would build a prototype to meet the specifications and the contract would be complete. A few scientists were employed for their "purely theoretical research" focus. Engineers worked closely with scientists to apply the research to products.

The Nature of Defense Contracts

Although the company had grown to 1,500 employees by 1995 and had some successful contracts, it had never realized its full profit potential. AVIONICS had a good reputation, however, for designing state-of-the-art electronic-sensing systems. From the mid-1970s to the late 1980s, defense contracts were such that engineers had the freedom to go above and beyond the original system specs and design better than specified systems. The government would pay for these additional costs through a system known as cost-plus (what it cost the company to make the product, plus a specified profit such as 3 percent).

Beginning in the late 1980s, the nature of contracts changed. While the companies still had to submit proposals and be competitively selected, now they had to be much more accurate about their costs because the government would no longer pay *any* cost plus profit. The company would only be paid the amount of its bid proposal. This meant that defense contractors had to anticipate the cost of designing a new system and had to manage costs if they expected a profit at the end of their contract. The role of project manager and other administrative functions began to take on a more significant position in AVIONICS as it struggled to contain costs and deliver on time.

Engineers, used to the creative "give them more than they asked for" design activities, struggled to adhere to the cost and schedule disciplines now imposed on them. Engineers felt frustrated as they were asked to coordinate more closely with each other and were told not to deliver more than promised in the contract. For some, the joy of their work was diminished as these restrictions became more and more common. In addition, many engineers complained that they did not understand what was expected of them. Trained as engineers and scientists and not as administrators, they felt confused about how to conduct business in this new environment.

Administrative overhead costs increased as administrators spent more time managing cost and schedule. Administrative overhead (AO) costs were critical to the bidding process. The lower the AO, the more successful a company would likely be in the bidding process for new contracts. AO was a function of the cost of facilities, administrators and executives, staffing, and other costs not directly related to a contract such as training, public relations, and security. AVIONICS AO was $32 per hour. Many smaller electronics firms had rates closer to $25 per hour.

When an engineer or scientist worked on a contract, he or she was required to record a job number on the weekly time card. The accounting department would track the job numbers, and that was how they kept track of each contract's costs. Whenever the employee did something that was not directly supportive of a contract, then his or her costs were charged to AO.

AVIONICS Current Business

As AVIONICS continued to struggle to reduce its AO cost, it sought additional ways to increase its profits. Top executives reasoned that, if they could take some of their technological advances in electronic-sensing systems to the commercial market, then they might realize greater profits. Consequently, in the early 1990s, the top executives began expecting each group within the company to find products that the public might want, and to take them commercial, if possible. The senior management team spent much of its time at its meetings discussing how this strategy should be able to help increase profits. They reasoned that if their products sold in the commercial markets, then they would be able partially to cover the costs of their highly paid engineers and scientists, and some AO costs. This would increase their ability to bid on defense contracts.

AVIONICS executives also tried one other new venture. They opened up a small facility near their current facility, transferred a few key administrators and engineers to it, and began seeking international opportunities. The new facility was necessary for two reasons. First, security of national defense products was paramount. The new facility would not house national defense secrets. Second, the facility would have a separate budget and, therefore, AO would be significantly reduced, which would allow them to bid more competitively for international business.

Groupware Fiasco

by Diane Fiero and Jonnetta Thomas-Chambers

Dr. Susan Pollard, dean of human sciences and humanities (HSH) at Southern University, wanted the HSH division office to operate smoothly and more efficiently. Since Dr. Pollard's role as dean demanded much of her time outside the office, she relied heavily on Dr. Eve Gordon, the new associate dean, to manage the office in her absence.

The dean and the staff were coping with many changes at the college. The president of the university had recently been promoted to chancellor and an acting president was temporarily assigned until the position was filled. The acting president immediately initiated some changes by demoting the associate vice president of academic affairs back to the faculty level and replacing him with the former associate dean of human sciences and humanities, the ex-wife of the former associate vice president. This left the vacancy within HSH, which was eventually filled by Dr. Eve Gordon, previously chair of humanities. Although the dean depended on Dr. Gordon to manage the office and staff in her absence, Dr. Gordon was reluctant to make any sudden changes in the department, even though they were desperately needed.

Since Dr. Pollard's priority was to ensure harmony at the HSH office, she decided to bring in a consulting team that had designed a groupware project, which they believed helped to improve communications and resolve conflict.

The Division Secretaries

Each division in the university had a secretarial staff in the division office and a supervising secretary for each of the four faculty suites. HSH was no different in this respect, with a staff of five secretaries in the division office and four suite secretaries. These two groups of secretaries had very different responsibilities and interacted infrequently. The suite secretaries would come to the division office twice daily to make photocopies and pick up mail, occasionally asking a division secretary for information on behalf of a student or faculty member. The division secretaries, also overloaded with work, would sometimes ask the suite secretaries to take on additional responsibilities, such as handling the paperwork for faculty searches and other long-term projects. Angela Sommers, the senior business coordinator for HSH and suite secretary supervisor, authorized all requests for help. The division office secretaries only went to her for help when they could not find help internally. Angela knew the workload of the suite secretaries, who supported 20 to 30 faculty members, was extremely heavy.

Problems and Conflicts

At some point, the requests of the division office secretaries became excessive and Angela felt that the distribution of secretarial work in the division needed improvement. She took her concerns to Dr. Pollard and explained that Martha Shipley, Dr. Gordon's secretary, was not doing her fair share of the work, and expressed that this was causing a significant amount of animosity and disruption among the secretarial staff. Angela proclaimed that the situation had intensified when Dr. Gordon took charge of managing the division office staff. Dr. Pollard promised to make the necessary changes to improve the environment in the division office.

This was not the first time Dr. Pollard received complaints about Martha's performance. Dr. Gordon's predecessor had disregarded Martha's complaints and expected an equal share of work from her. In comparison, Dr. Gordon took Martha's complaints very seriously and would redistribute Martha's work, increasing the other secretaries' workload, so that Martha was not overburdened. Dr. Pollard felt that Dr. Gordon's intentions were to maintain harmony and respond to an employee's plea, but the results of Dr. Gordon's actions magnified animosity within the office staff.

Each secretary in the division office had been given assignments from Martha's desk at some point. Hostility and rage reflected the secretaries' feelings. Cries like, "What is Martha's job anyway?" and "What exactly does she do?" were asserted. They eventually resented anyone who asked them for the slightest favor, including the suite secretaries, who usually only called them in an emergency. The "it's not my job" attitude pervaded the division office and un' ermined any team effort. Each person was out to protect herself from additional work. The other secretaries wanted to communicate their feelings about the problems in the office but feared being perceived, by Dr. Gordon, as uncooperative or instigating. So all of the secretaries kept their complaints about Martha to themselves and vented their feelings to those they felt safe talking to, namely, each other.

The ages of the women in the group ranged from 25 to 60. Danielle, one of the suite secretaries in HSH, supported 28 faculty members. She enjoyed her job immensely because it allowed her a lot of independence. Danielle interacted with the remainder of the departments' support staff on occasion, mostly for information regarding appointments with the dean, book orders, and scheduling events. At some point, Danielle, too, was given work from Martha's desk. She also served as a sounding board when staff members complained to her about Martha.

The Groupware Fiasco

The groupware project that Dr. Pollard considered had proven effective elsewhere as an intervention used to resolve office conflict. However, this process required participation from all levels and competent leadership and facilitation. Some felt the groupware project did not contain either of these essential elements. The facilitator was an astute computer programmer but lacked expertise in organizational development and communication.

Still, in March 1996, the administration of HSH decided that the secretarial staff would attend a series of groupware software sessions. The dean felt that an environment that provided anonymity for airing complaints would help facilitate conversation and possibly unearth solutions for the group's interpersonal conflicts. The secretaries' reactions were mixed. Some seemed excited about the class and hoped it would help relieve tension in the office, while others did not see the point, nor did they have the time to spend away from the office.

"Did you two see the e-mail message from the dean?" Martha asked Betty and Maureen who were waiting in line to use the copier.

"I sure did, and I think it is a great idea," replied Betty.

"Personally I don't know why they bother. I am too busy to waste two hours every Friday, for a month, arguing. Besides, our jobs are very different and the administration won't listen to our suggestions anyway. We will have sat through this whole process and nothing will change, you wait and see," stated Maureen with a huff.

The facilitator used the groupware software in the following manner:

The division office and suite secretaries were brought together in a room with tables and computer terminals positioned in the shape of a horseshoe.

The facilitator and a large screen were stationed at the open end of the horseshoe.

Each person was seated at a computer terminal and then asked a series of questions.

Their typed responses, disguising the respondent, appeared on the screen at the front of the room for all participants to see.

The facilitator asked the group what they perceived as problems in the division.

The participants typed responses like, "I think there is a lack of communication in the office," and "There is not enough teamwork."

Once everyone entered their information, the facilitator constructed a list of the most commonly cited responses. For example, responses indicating lack of communication were cited three times, so it became the number-one problem on the list.

All problems were eventually listed and then examined individually. First to be addressed was the lack of communication. The facilitator asked the participants to suggest ways the division could communicate better. Again the participants responded anonymously by typing in their suggestions. The facilitator compiled a list of the most common responses.

The process was designed to continue until all problems were discussed and solutions had been reached.

These results would then be compiled by the facilitator, outlined in a formal report, and given to all participants and Dr. Pollard.

This process had one main advantage—it encouraged a greater quantity of input, and some had much more to say than others.

However, there were many disadvantages, including the following:

One disadvantage was social pressure. When one person would complain about a topic, others would tag along and say, "I definitely agree with comment 6." Ultimately, participants took sides over various topics.

The tasks structured in the groupware sessions were not interdependent: that is, each person typed in front of her computer without interacting with others; therefore, the session provided little opportunity for teamwork and cohesion.

There was a two-month lapse in time before the final report was distributed.

Upon its distribution, the group had concerns about accuracy.

Anonymity was not exactly maintained and led to some interpersonal conflict. During the groupware process, Danielle had formed some opinions and aired them anonymously. However, as the process continued it was fairly obvious that anonymity had been lost. Danielle felt that it wasn't difficult to tell where comments came from, especially when everyone knew who was the last to type. Though Danielle believed the group enjoyed the first session, further sessions had poor results. She recalled an instance when the leader asked for possible solutions to the problems in the department. Someone typed, "We need a man to be in charge of the department." The statement hung there like an anvil waiting to drop. Danielle, the youngest and most outspoken, typed a question that asked what was meant by the comment. The respondent conveyed that men and women differed and that she preferred working for a man. Danielle was stunned and typed in a response stating that she did not feel that gender was of importance when selecting a manager. At that point, with the male facilitator flustered and unsure how to proceed, Danielle was convinced that the groupware software had met its match. Furthermore, everyone deduced who input both messages and, as mentioned earlier, the veil of anonymity had been lifted. Martha wanted a male boss and Danielle disagreed.

Outcomes of the Groupware Project

The following week discussions focused on the group's last session and subject matter. A lot of finger pointing went on and the woman who entered the remark was very defensive. Danielle remembered a conversation with a couple of the secretaries.

"Well, you sure tweaked Martha during our session," one secretary stated.

"Yeah, maybe you should have toned down your response a little, Danielle," chimed in another.

Danielle responded by explaining that she had worked with men and women bosses and declared that, typically, the working styles of the subordinates, not the boss, is what changes. Danielle added that it was unlikely that the dean would step down because she was not a man, and that Martha would have to get over it. Danielle maintained that Martha's sexist view was unacceptable. Danielle wondered how Martha could devalue the two women who had helped her achieve and retain the position she had with the college.

Danielle rationalized that the differences in perceptions were based on age. Danielle, 25, was junior to the other secretaries, all over 55. The majority had worked for men during their careers and, perhaps, working for a woman challenged their belief systems. Danielle, born after the women's rights movement flourished in the 1960s, believed that a woman could hold the same position as a man and do a superb job.

At the time of the groupware activity, Danielle was a senior at the college, majoring in psychology and sociology, and the leader of many on-campus organizations that focused on equality. Danielle had just been accepted into a graduate program at a prestigious university and the focus of her graduate studies was to be Women in Corporate America. Danielle admitted that these circumstances probably influenced how she reacted to Martha's comment. Danielle empathized with Martha's position and respected her right to her opinion, but decided to agree to disagree.

In the weeks that remained, participants grudgingly completed the sessions and compiled their suggestions for the final administrative report. After the report was handed over to the dean and associate dean, a meeting was called. Administration demonstrated concern about the other issues that had been communicated but gently sidestepped the gender comment. Eventually, the report and its contents faded. It wasn't long before the dean announced her retirement. All changes to the department were placed on hold until a successor could be found and everyone settled back into their old ways. Eventually, tensions over the sessions cooled and were even laughed at later.

Incident on the USS *Whitney*

by Jeff Balesh

Ensign Beck sat in the old, executive-type chair in his cramped office and felt as if he had been hit over the head with a baseball bat. His experiences up to this point on the USS *Whitney* were rocky, to say the least, but had not been as bad as the blow he had just taken. Now, he felt he had a day to mark on the calendar as the darkest one in his short career in the U.S. Navy. However, not only was he sure that he had done the right thing, two older officers supported him. Still, the beating he had just taken was a difficult one to stomach.

USS *Whitney*

The USS *Whitney* was a "precommissioning" vessel, a ship that hadn't been put into service yet (or "commissioned"). It was being built in a shipyard in San Diego, California. There were still about 10 more months before the ship would be in the hands of the Navy. Because the ship was still just a hulk of keel and iron ribs, the coed crew (about 90 percent men at this point) worked on an ugly, dilapidated green barge docked a pier down from the burgeoning vessel. There were about 40 members who had already reported to the unit out of the 560 who would eventually make up the crew.

Ensign Beck was a member of the supply department, the unit on the ship that was in charge of all of the ship's financial dealings as well as all the services for the crew. These responsibilities included functions such as payroll, the sale of retail merchandise, the ordering of supplies, and the monitoring of the ship's budget. The person in charge of the supply department was Lieutenant Commander (Lt. Cdr.) Fuller, a 13-year officer who was known to be a stern disciplinarian. Although he had stated many times thus far in his stint as the supply department head (commonly referred to as "Suppo" in Navy lingo) that the number-one priority of any officer's job was to take care of his or her people, he was decidedly harsh on his officer subordinates. Even though his harsh style affected his subordinates' feelings toward him, they could not deny that he had a good reputation for running ships' supply departments.

Emblematic Merchandise Giveaway

Ensign Beck served as the sales officer, his first real job in the Navy. He was to be in charge of the ship's store, laundry, barbershop, and post office once the crew moved on board the ship. On board the barge, he supervised a unit of eight personnel that, in addition to running a fabricated barber operation, had as its primary responsibility a barge version of the ship's store. Ensign Beck was also responsible for preparing for operations on board the ship many months in the future. At this point, the sales operation primarily sold what were called emblematic items. This referred to anything with the ship's name on it, including such items as ball caps, shirts, coffee mugs, lighters, and the like.

The rules and regulations on a precommissioning ship were less stringent than those on a commissioned ship. The circumstances and regulations surrounding certain aspects of the operation of the store, such as how inventory was stored, sold, and accounted for, were not as restrictive as that of a store on board an active ship. However, keeping solid accountability of inventory and money was still of primary importance. Ensign Beck's job performance, as well as that of Suppo Lt. Cdr. Fuller, could be harmed by a critical loss in inventory or money.

Sometimes, the ship's commanding officer, Captain Gramm, took emblematic merchandise on public affairs trips either to sell or, more likely, to give away. On these trips, the captain did most of the public speaking and glad-handing and the Suppo was his right-hand man. However, Lt. Cdr. Fuller never let opportunities go by without doing his share of hobnobbing. This meant that he gave away his share of merchandise as well.

As a result of these sojourns, the sales division was forced to try to make up for the lost inventory due to the giveaways. In order to overcome this accounting nightmare, Ensign Beck wrote up itemized inventories of goods given away at these functions to have Lt. Cdr. Fuller sign in order to write off the losses. The amounts of the write-offs were usually small, in the realm of $50 or less, but significant enough to have to account for them. To put these losses into perspective, the size of the adjustments was about one-sixteenth the amount of monthly revenue (about $800) at the time.

As long as Ensign Beck had a signature on one of these statements, it technically absolved him of accountability. However, it was still an accounting headache; furthermore, it cheated the crew out of money that should have gone for the benefit of the crew's Morale, Welfare, and Recreation fund, which received the profits realized by sales. Not to be forgotten in this process of writing off lost inventory was the chore of requesting Lt. Cdr. Fuller to sign one of these sheets because it required asking a service from him. Since he and the captain gave away the merchandise, they were responsible for the shortages for which Ensign Beck had to account. Yet, Ensign Beck still had the feeling that the Suppo retained the power to deny the request if he so desired. Although this had not happened, the ensign was used to routine bouts of questioning regarding other matters he brought up for the Suppo's approval.

About six months after Ensign Beck had reported to the unit, he sat in his office braced for the aftereffects of a particularly high-level public relations trip. The supply officer and captain had gone to Bremerton, Washington, the location where the ship was to be commissioned as well as homeported, to meet with the commissioning committee—the group in charge of raising money for the commissioning event. It was an important time in the ship's short life span so it was critical at this point to generate as much money and support as possible. Therefore, Ensign Beck knew that a significant amount of merchandise would be given away. Sure enough, both the captain and the supply officer distributed *gratis* several ball caps and other items during the trip.

Two Lieutenants

Now, the young ensign was forced to try to determine how much was given away. This task was made more difficult because the notes taken to document what was sold, what was given away, and who still owed money for items were incomplete and hard to decipher. In order to try to complete the story, he plied people's recollections as to what transpired. He eventually came up with a tally of items that had to be accounted for.

He brought the itemized list to Lieutenant (Lt.) Frank Wilson's attention. Lt. Wilson, in charge of ordering supplies for the ship, was a 17-year Navy man who spent his first 10 years in an enlisted status. He had much respect among the whole crew, including the supply officer and captain, as he had the reputation of being a "doer" and a go-getter who never failed to have a witty comment perfectly delivered to deflate any tense situation. He befriended Ensign Beck when they first met on a visit Lt. Wilson made to Navy Supply Corps School while Ensign Beck was still a student there. Lt. Wilson also had assumed the role as Ensign Beck's mentor when they were together in the unit. As such, he acted as a buffer between Ensign Beck and the Suppo. He fulfilled this role well as he not only was a wily veteran of various tours throughout his career but was also respected by the Suppo. However, the Suppo did not hesitate, when threatened, to let him and everyone else know who was in charge.

Lt. Cathy Smith was also informed of the situation. This was her first tour on a ship that would be at sea. It was an established fact in the Navy that officers, and everyone else for that matter in seagoing careers, proved their mettle in tours at sea. Thus, she hadn't really been tested yet as an officer. Nevertheless, she was the assistant supply officer, second in charge in the department, not only because she could afford the time to dedicate to this administrative role (due to the fact that the department that she would be heading did not have a role as of yet), but also because she had more years as an officer (eight) than Lt. Wilson had (seven).

Lt. Wilson advised Ensign Beck to write up an itemized sheet for the Suppo to sign. To do this was nothing new; however, for the first time, he advised the ensign to also take it up to the captain to sign. Lt. Smith, as she was inclined to do, agreed with him. By having the captain sign the sheet, Ensign Beck's absolution of responsibility would not only be solidified, but it would also notify the captain of what was involved with giving these items away, especially when the Suppo was involved. Ensign Beck knew at the time that it was a way not only for himself but also for the other officers to get back at the Suppo, and he agreed to it partly for that reason.

Lt. Cdr. Fuller was not someone who would be called a genuinely kind man, and every officer in the department had suffered to a certain extent by serving under such a leader, including Ensign Beck. About three months after reporting, the Suppo had seated the ensign in his office and told him he had better improve his performance or else. Ensign Beck didn't know what exactly would happen to him, beyond poor fitness reports, but he knew it would be unsavory, whatever it was. That was the way it was with the Suppo: One didn't really know how he would do it, but you knew it would be bad. At any rate, although Ensign Beck knew he was taking a risk in challenging the Suppo's authority by essentially "telling on him" to the captain, he willfully agreed to take the chance as he knew he had the support of the two older officers in his department.

"Telling On" the Suppo

So Ensign Beck wrote up the sheet with separate blocks for the Suppo and the captain to sign. He showed the Suppo the sheet of paper and told him that he would be taking it up to the captain for his signature. The Suppo leaned back in his chair with his hands on the back of his head in a relaxed gesture and, wearing a Cheshire cat grin that was his trademark and that bled with condescension, said, "Go ahead. See what he says."

On the *Whitney*, as it was throughout the Navy, norms played a big role in dictating acceptable forms of behavior, including relations between seniors and subordinates. Norms such as walking to the left of a senior officer and behind a couple of paces and asking permission to join the meal table were well entrenched in every officer's mind. However, these norms were easy to follow; they were pretty cut-and-dried. A more complicated area was the chain of command and the norms that governed the relationships within this hierarchical structure. These norms, mainly concerned with respecting the primacy of the chain so as to take things that concerned superiors to one's immediate supervisor before it went any further, were taken very seriously by everyone, especially the top echelon of leadership. They provided the backbone for this foundation of military operations. By allowing the ensign to proceed, he was in effect giving the ensign permission to ignore the norm of sticking to the hierarchy and in so doing cleared the way for him to visit the captain on his own.

The Captain's Response

With the Suppo's blessing, Ensign Beck took the sheet up to the captain. Captain Gramm had been in the Navy for 27 years. He started off as an enlisted man, and served in this status in the Vietnam War. The *Whitney* was the fifth vessel to be under his command and he was looking forward to this tour as it would be his last shot at a promotion to admiral. Although he was a stern man and could "undress a person down to his underwear," he had taken a liking to Ensign Beck. This was due to several reasons, not the least of which was that his uncle had played on the football team with George Gipp (of "win one for the Gipper" fame) at Notre Dame, Ensign Beck's alma mater.

After Capt. Gramm read what was on the sheet, he remarked that if it weren't for the Suppo's glad-handing of all his supply officer buddies, there wouldn't be such a loss. He wrote a sarcastic note on the sheet underneath his signature noting something to this effect. He read it to Ensign Beck with a malicious grin. From moments like this one, it appeared that he enjoyed taunting the Suppo. Although he was fully aware of the quality of Lt. Cdr. Fuller's work, it seemed that he took merciless delight in "spinning him up."

The Suppo's Response

Ensign Beck delivered this note to the Suppo. Because the captain had written the note for Fuller, Ensign Beck was obligated to show the note to him. He actually didn't expect the note to be that big of a deal; as a matter of fact, maybe the Suppo would see the humor in all of it. After all, it was mostly true; but as the Suppo's eyes looked at the note, Ensign Beck witnessed the progression of blood rushing to his face. He could tell he was getting angry, and the pressure was building up inside of him like that of a teakettle rising quickly to the boiling point. The Suppo violently jumped up from his chair, pointed to the outside of the barge, and yelled, "Outside!" When they reached the outside of the barge, Lt. Cdr. Fuller proceeded to berate the young ensign like no one had done before or since. "How can you f--- me!?! You don't know what the hell you're doing! Why can't you trust me? I've been in this organization for, how many years?" He didn't dare answer the question and he didn't need to. "For almost 15 years! Don't you think I know what I'm doing? Do you think I would totally screw you?" Again, Ensign Beck did not answer. "Damn it, Ensign!" And this is how it went for a good 10 minutes: Fuller yelling at the top of his lungs and Beck standing there shell-shocked. The Suppo's veins were bulging out of his neck, he was gesticulating wildly with his arms. It soon became a surreal moment. The young officer, just a year and a half out of the ignorant bliss that marked his experience in college, took himself out of the present and wondered, "Why am I here? Why did I screw myself by getting into this mess?" He wanted to watch this event, detached, with no emotional involvement, but he had never felt such animosity toward a human being in his life.

When Lt. Cdr. Fuller finished with his diatribe, he stormed back into the barge. Ensign Beck, stunned, went back into his office, a mere few feet across the hall from Suppo's office. Everyone on the forward end of the barge must have heard all the yelling. Lts. Wilson and Andersen came into Ensign Beck's office to see what had happened, and to offer their support. The ensign sat in his chair dazed. The two senior officers reiterated their understanding of what the ensign had done and expressed their disbelief at what had just transpired. The Suppo eventually came into Ensign Beck's office after about 20 minutes—during which time he must have forced himself to cool down.

He apologized for getting so out of hand, and talked to the young officer in a much calmer manner while his voice was still firm, but now marked with a tone of pleading. "I am sorry for yelling like that. I shouldn't do that, and I know it. But . . ." ("There was always a 'but' with him," Ensign Beck thought) "you have to understand why I do these things. It's not to screw anyone; it's to do what I think is right. You must trust me with this stuff. I know what I'm doing."

Ensign Beck, a subordinate, had no choice but to accept his apology and his reasons for being upset, at least to his face.

Insubordination or Unclear Loyalties?

by Asbjorn Osland, George Fox University,
and Shannon Shoul

Background

Omega House was established for those terminally ill patients who needed to find inner peace and dignity as well as the best in hospice care in their remaining days. It had been started by a group that had been unable to sustain it financially and it had gone bankrupt and been closed for several years. Then, in the early 1990s, the Social Action Consortium (SAC) agreed to assume responsibility for it. It became one of many services provided by SAC, which brought together 17 different groups, including small social service agencies and donor organizations that wished to be involved in more direct service than contributing to a funding agency. For nearly 80 years, it provided service to the less fortunate and disenfranchised. It provided a wide range of services, in addition to Omega House, including assorted special projects in the field of education, services to at-risk youth, shelters and apartments for those with special needs, services for people with HIV, addictions counseling, an inner-city health program and emergency food assistance, consumer credit seminars, and political advocacy for issues that affected the poor and disenfranchised. Its expenditures and revenues in 1995 were roughly $8 million.

Program Director

Ellen didn't get much sleep. When she had been a full-time nurse, she used to fall asleep immediately after an exhausting but satisfying shift; she could leave the problems at work. However, now that she had become a program manager at Omega House, she found that things tended to nag at her and keep her awake. Like today, one of her employees, George, seemed to be insubordinate. She would never have spoken to her superior in that tone. Why did he think he could get away with it with her? She wondered if she appeared unsure of herself. Was George confused over where his loyalties should lie?

Ellen began working at the hospice as a registered nurse in patient care five years ago. Almost three years later, after her predecessor had been dismissed, she became the temporary program director and assumed the managerial responsibilities for Omega House, in addition to clinical oversight of patient care. Given her lack of managerial experience at the time of her temporary assignment, she had been promised managerial training by SAC but after two years was still waiting. Ellen felt very comfortable dealing with clinical care and was fortunate to have a strong clinical staff, an excellent and devoted kitchen crew, and a dedicated volunteer coordinator, who organized the extensive services provided by the volunteers. However, she was less comfortable with her managerial duties in relation to SAC. Also, the troubled financial history of the Omega House concerned her. To further complicate matters, the SAC administration had proven both arbitrary and autocratic in Ellen's experience. Though she had suffered through the bankruptcy, she missed the lean administrative structure Omega House had enjoyed before the bankruptcy and subsequent SAC ownership. Her clinical staff had also worked at Omega House before SAC assumed control and were often skeptical of SAC-mandated changes.

Additionally, she was not quite certain what George, Omega's new development officer, was doing. Immediately before SAC's executive director, Patti Kelley, left to take another job with a prominent ecumenical relief organization, she had hired George. This left the organization without an executive director, as the governing board had decided to take some time to fill the leadership position. George seemed to spend most of his time with the other development people at SAC, working on the cross-program task force on fundraising. He was the only one with professional fundraising experience, and many within SAC viewed him as an expert. Ellen understood that should George obtain a large donation or grant for SAC, it could also help Omega House. However, it had been her experience that she had to fight hard for resources. Thus, when George had been assigned to her, she thought he would focus most of his attention on Omega House. Ellen understood that Omega House was one of SAC's only programs with active volunteers who could raise funds. Thus, she understood that George could also be useful to other parts of SAC, but still felt that since George had been hired with money from a development grant previously given to Omega House, he should spend the bulk of his time serving their needs. Funds from this development grant had also been used to purchase office equipment used by George and others.

Ellen had also come to understand, based on gossip, that George's past job history involved a personal indiscretion that had led to his termination with another employer. This made it difficult for her to trust him completely.

What's George Up To?

Ellen entered the kitchen early Monday morning and said, "Hi, Dan. What's for breakfast today?"

Dan, with his back to her, was gyrating to the rhythm of a CD blaring in the boom box. Dan's wide-ranging preferences for music ran from the church hymns he played on Sunday evenings to punk. Ellen was not quite certain where this particular CD fit on the continuum but took the liberty of turning it down. Dan turned and noted her presence, "Oh, hi, you old bitty—don't you like my music? I suppose you'd prefer MUSAK," he responded in a playfully scornful tone. He then approached her and hugged her, stating, "It's nice to see you. What's up?" Their relationship represented the friendliness existing throughout the Omega staff: approachable, playful, and comfortable.

While attempting to wrap her arms around Dan's ample upper body, Ellen looked over his shoulder and noted a tray of long-stemmed glasses sitting on the counter in the dishwashing area and asked, "Who passed on?" The long-stemmed glasses were used by the staff to honor the patients who died. The average stay was only three weeks. To avoid developing the lack of feeling that one can find in service settings where people routinely suffered tragedy, the staff engaged in this ceremony each time someone died; they left a light on outside the person's room and shared a toast of a nonalcoholic sparkling beverage.

"Theo. He had been active all weekend. Fortunately, his immediate family was with him last night," Dan responded soberly. "Active" meant Theo had been showing the physical reactions that were symptomatic of impending death.

They both paused a moment before continuing. The customary, "That's too bad," did not seem to fit, as it was a hospice designated for people with terminal cancer or AIDS who were near death upon admission.

Ellen continued, "Say, what time did George come in on Friday? I was at the SAC office for a meeting. He usually comes through the kitchen. Did you happen to notice?"

Dan looked out the window and thought, "Let's see. I had finished breakfast and was outside having a cigarette. It must have been after 9 o'clock. He seems to come at about that time, except for a couple of times a week when he comes in while I'm doing the breakfast dishes, which would make it after 10:30."

Ellen thanked Dan and went to the portion of the old estate house where the patients were located. Her office was immediately behind the nursing station. She liked to be close to the action and sometimes wondered if she was cut out for chasing after administrative staff, like George, who wasn't communicating regularly with her.

That morning she dealt with the customary managerial concerns for the first half hour and spent the balance of the morning reviewing the financial statements in preparation for the budget meeting the next day. She noted that while SAC's development efforts had seemed to improve funding for Omega, Omega's own fundraising efforts had resulted in little change from the previous year, when they didn't even have their own development officer. Now that they had George, she had expected Omega's contributions to rise. She also noticed that George's salary was charged to a grant, destined in its entirety to Omega's budget. She thought to herself, "If George is working for Omega, these numbers ought to be changing. Since he's charged to Omega, I really should be more aware of what he's up to." She resolved to speak with George that afternoon.

Confrontation

Ellen walked up the stairs of the main portion of the house to the office, directly above the kitchen and Dan's blaring boom box, where George worked. She found him at the photocopy machine. When he saw her, he looked somewhat sheepish. Ellen noted that the yellow copies looked like flyers; she caught a glimpse of the image of a canoe, and the words "Boundary Waters Adventure" before he hastily scooped the copies up, and put them in the opened briefcase positioned unsteadily on top of the photocopy machine. "Just taking a few minutes to make some personal copies—I brought in my own ream of yellow paper. I hope you don't mind," said George, averting her gaze. He then cleared his throat and proceeded, "What can I do for you?"

"I don't want you making hundreds of copies on our machine. The paper is a minor expense, but the copies are not. It's leased and we pay several cents per copy," said Ellen as forcefully as she could without shouting. She had not wanted their meeting to begin this way.

"Understood," responded George quickly. He continued, "I'd be happy to reimburse SAC for the copies. I've done 300."

"That would be nice," responded Ellen before continuing. She paused briefly while he closed his briefcase and went to his office. She followed him and took a seat after he gestured to her to sit in the chair customarily occupied by the university intern, Lisa, who was off at a retreat for her university. Trying to change the mood from a disciplinary one, which she felt she had been forced into, to the collaborative tone she had intended, Ellen continued, "I wanted to compliment you again on the 'casino night' last week. It went well, and I've received several calls from people who attended." She was referring to a fundraising event they had held the previous week; it was an evening on the lawn where the sponsors, volunteers, and staff played various casino-like games. She wanted to begin with something positive, even though she had discovered that Lisa had a larger role in the arrangements than she would have expected from an intern.

George responded, "Well, that's what I'm here for."

Fundraising was a big issue with Omega and SAC. Some of the low-profile SAC programs had been cut recently. Ellen had been told by SAC that her program would not be cut but was concerned nonetheless, since she wanted to upgrade some of their equipment as well as complete the remodeling of the facility. To do so, she needed more money, and George had been recruited for that purpose.

Additionally, some of Ellen's uncertainty stemmed from the autocratic style Patti, the former SAC director, had used to manage the various programs. Sometimes Patti had seemed capricious in how she would arbitrarily fire program directors. Ellen also had regarded her as insensitive; Patti would come in, unannounced, leading a delegation of visitors through the facility. Since Omega was a hospice, Ellen felt that such visits should have been handled with greater sensitivity. Patti had also tried to micromanage many of the programs. She would make decisions about minutiae, sometimes change programs without consulting the program director, and involve staff from the various programs in SAC issues, such as the cross-program task force on fundraising. Ellen understood that this was a large concern for SAC, and she knew that George, who was assigned to Omega, needed to participate in this fundraising task force. However, Ellen was concerned that Omega's internal fundraising efforts were not getting the attention they deserved from George. It was apparent to Ellen that Lisa, the student intern, had assumed a leadership role, filling the vacuum left by George. However, Lisa was temporary and should not supplant George.

With this in mind, Ellen then asked, "I was wondering how it was going with the Omega committee you're leading for fundraising?" Ellen had formed an internal committee, comprised of both staff and volunteers (some of whom were donors), to generate ideas for fundraising. She had heard from committee members that George was difficult to communicate with and frequently did not attend the meetings. Still, Ellen was aware of how both the staff and volunteers comprised a group that had been together for years, and that it would be difficult for George to be accepted immediately.

George stood up and loomed over Ellen who was still seated. He stated assertively and loudly, "Look, I can't get the job done if I'm to work in committees all the time here and at SAC." He continued to look directly at Ellen in a challenging manner.

Ellen responded quickly and decisively, "I asked you to be on that committee and I expected you to participate. These people have been a part of Omega for years and can contribute a great deal both in service and ideas. Those who are donors also provide a lot of financial support. They are the ones who keep us going. You can't ignore them. Furthermore, they need your fundraising expertise. I know it's difficult to enter an established group, but you won't have a chance if they don't perceive you as more cooperative."

George responded, still hostile, but more carefully this time after noting Ellen's displeasure, "I had no intention of leaving anyone out of the loop, or avoiding the committee. It's just that I'm part of SAC's cross-program task force. I had a few conflicts and I had to decide where to focus my energies. I felt I had to do what SAC wanted."

Ellen stood and walked around the room. She listened, thought for a moment, and then responded, "I understand that you need to coordinate your Omega efforts with the SAC team's overall development plans and may be asked to do things with them. However, when I tell you specifically what to do, I expect you to do it."

George responded tersely, "Maybe you should speak with the SAC development officer so that we can all understand our jobs better."

Ellen felt she was not getting through to George. She stated, "You're assigned here. Your salary comes out of my budget. I don't see the confusion. Yes, I'll speak with the SAC development officer to clarify what it is I told you to do and why I want you to do it. But that won't change that you're working here for me. So please do what I say."

Ellen felt that she couldn't have been more explicit. However, later, on her way home, she wondered if the problem was structural rather than individual. George reported to her and to SAC's development chief. She recalled how SAC's development chief sat in on George's interview with her and lobbied for George because of his skills, which he said would round out SAC's development team. Thus, she wondered, "Is the problem George, and what appears to be his irresponsible and noncommunicative behavior, or is it confusion over who is to direct his efforts, or both?"

Leading TQM in Panama

by Asbjorn Osland, George Fox University

Overview

Jim had returned to Panama, where he had worked the previous two years (1990–1992) as the company human resources (HR) manager. He had just conducted interviews to better understand research he had done earlier. Jim wondered how the latest company-change program, total quality management (TQM), would fare. He asked himself, "How can TQM be adopted in these old, company-town operations of the Tropical Export Company? How can one expect participation to flourish when the leaders are so autocratic?"

The Tropical Export Company was a family-controlled, North American–based, multinational corporation. It had very extensive production operations in Latin America, which produced a labor-intensive, tropical export product for industrialized markets, mainly North America and Europe. There were a number of production divisions spread throughout Central and South America, but Punta Blanca and Palo Amarillo were the ones Jim had served.

Both were remote small company towns; the production divisions and towns had the same names. They were backwater towns that had developed because of the production divisions of the company. There were a handful of professionals (i.e., lawyers and doctors) that serviced the local populations, but many of the residents were blue-collar workers, who had some connection to the company. Many of the employees came from families that had worked for the company for several generations. The average tenure among the more than 12,000 employees of the company was 13 years, and it was not uncommon to find veterans with over 30 years of service. People spoke of the company with a mixture of loyalty and wariness, the latter due to the ongoing tension between the strong unions and management. In the past, the company had established the infrastructure (i.e., company stores, schools, hospitals, roads, water and power grids) of the towns. However, most of these services had been turned over to the private sector, in terms of the company store, or the government. Nevertheless, the company towns still had a total institution feel about them, where one's status within the company figured prominently in one's position within the community as well. Punta Blanca was located on the Pacific side of Panama, and Palo Amarillo on the Caribbean. Palo Amarillo had a mix of English-speaking blacks, various Native American tribes, and Latins. Punta Blanca was predominantly Latin. The company provided housing to thousands of workers.

Punta Blanca

Jim arrived in the late afternoon and found he needed to wait until the next day to speak to Julian, the general manager. He had dinner with another visitor at the guesthouse where he was staying—a Latino information systems expert, now assigned to the corporate office in the United States. After chatting and watching TV, they decided to walk to the wharf to watch the loading process.

From the wharf, Jim's companion, who had spent many years working at Punta Blanca early in his career, told him, "See those houses there." He pointed to the modest wooden homes that lined the beach area. "That's where the Latinos lived. Only Americans and Europeans lived in the houses in the area surrounding the guesthouse. That's where the managers and supervisors now live. As late as 1970, there wasn't a single Latino manager or high-level supervisor."

Jim was surprised that he spoke with no bitterness. His companion had no doubt suffered from the "line," as they called it. The "line" referred to the social barrier to promotions of Latinos, erected during the 70-year neocolonial era when the company had dominated politics in the region. Jim hated to admit it, but he enjoyed the deference that remained for foreign managers within the company. His companion added, "You know that Julian is the first general manager from the region—the first one to cross the line." They then returned to the guesthouse to retire for the night.

Jim enjoyed staying in the guesthouse at Punta Blanca. He enjoyed the camaraderie he felt with the other guests—people he had known when he worked for the company. The next morning, after he awakened to the blast of the ship's horn as it began its journey to Europe with cargo the Tropical Export Company produced in Punta Blanca, Jim prepared to see Julian. He left the comfortable guesthouse and made his way to the office. The shade of the old avocado and mango trees cooled the sidewalk and protected passers-by from the blazing tropical sun. It occurred to Jim that the shade was analogous to the strong traditions of the Punta Blanca operation that buffered it from the more trendy, and ill-considered, managerial innovations suggested by the corporate headquarters.

Julian

Julian, the general manager of Punta Blanca, was native to the company town. He was educated in the United States, and completed a degree in the sciences. Early in his career he moved from research into production, where he spent nearly his entire career of more than 25 years.

Jim entered the office and greeted the secretaries. They explained that Julian was in the meeting room addressing his direct reports and other high-level subordinates, and that he should walk in and sit down. Jim slipped into the meeting room. Though in midsentence, Julian stopped and said, "Good morning, Jim." The others followed suit, and Jim took a seat in the rear of the room. Julian, a large, fit man, continued, waving his arms and addressing those in the meeting with a booming voice, "Though we've trained over 500 people in communication and the basics of TQM, I'm surprised that it has taken so long for you, the quality council, to get rolling. For two years, I've sat here and observed, but you've done nothing. Now, I'm going to leave and Jose is going to take charge. You will remain here until you all agree on what you should do and how you will proceed. I will no longer observe, because you've done next to nothing." Jose was the second-in-command, serving in the role of production manager. This was a position the company used to groom future general managers.

With that, he left, and gestured to Jim to accompany him. He was somewhat agitated and walked briskly to his office. On his way, he said to the secretary, "Could you please bring us some coffee?" Jim had seen him like this in the past and had felt somewhat intimidated—in the eyes of his 5,500 subordinates, Julian controlled the destiny of the operation. Yet Jim knew he could confront him, as he had done when Julian and the operations vice president had been poised to take aggressive action against some former subcontractors, who had signed with the competition. At that time, Jim, when he was still the HR manager, had encouraged Julian to avoid reacting emotionally in a way that could provoke a violent response on the part of the gun-slinging inhabitants of the area. Julian was a very savvy politician, and his finely honed political sensitivity prevailed over his more primal aggressive nature.

Jim gulped, while averting Julian's gaze, and said, "Does it seem at all ironic to you that you've just ordered them to be more participatory?"

Julian's eyes flashed for a moment, but he calmly responded, "Look, you're a good man, but sometimes you don't know squat about us." Still standing, he smiled and walked around to the back of Jim, strongly squeezed Jim's shoulder, and moved to his desk. "Excuse me for a moment while I make a few calls to the VP and corporate. Stay here or someone else will come in and we'll never get to talk."

Jim sat, sipped his coffee, and glanced at some publications on the coffee table. One was the local public relations document from the company's plastics and packaging subsidiary. The Tropical Export Company used so much plastic and packaging in its production and packaging operations that it had vertically integrated and had purchased a regional producer. Jim had visited them in Panama City from time to time during his tenure as the HR manager. They functioned in a largely autonomous fashion but were owned by the Tropical Export Company.

Jim reflected on his last visit to the plastics division in Panama City. Mario, the second-in-command as the manufacturing manager, had explained to Jim about their approach to TQM, "We get together with the general manager only when we're ready to. I lead the committee, but the participants feel free to argue with me. I provide direction, yet I'm not the ultimate authority. Then when we have something to suggest, we invite the general manager in, but only at that stage. If we invite him in too soon, he'll take over and people won't argue, because he's the boss."

Julian concluded his brief phone calls and sat down while addressing Jim, "So what questions do you want to ask me?"

Jim began, "I guess I have trouble understanding how participation will flourish in Punta Blanca."

Julian responded, "One has little to fear from participation. If you know the business, you can help people problem solve in a manner that enables them to develop. By giving people authority, they will come to you and seek your input. This gives me more power than I would have if I simply told an obedient work group what to do. I want people seeking answers. However, if I already know the answer, I don't ask them—I tell them what I want done. I guess what I like most is getting a large organization to do what I want it to do. I see TQM as a chance to try something new. It's a tool for me. At the start, I was encouraged by gringo consultants to push my direct reports to take more initiative in the quality council, and to be more accepting of cross-functional teams. However, I've refused to rush things. I know I could beat them over the head and, like good soldiers, they'd do what I want. However, I could be transferred at any time, and TQM would stop if they didn't assume ownership."

Jim was puzzled by this comment for what he had just observed in the meeting room seemed to reflect pushing. The secretary then knocked and entered, "The plane is waiting for you, Don Jim. It's going to Palo Amarillo, and you're on the roster." *Don* is a term of respect commonly used by Latinos when addressing men to whom they wish to show deference. With that, Jim bid farewell to Julian and rushed to the landing strip. Jim was to interview Robert, the general manager of Palo Amarillo.

Robert

Robert was born in the Caribbean and spent his early childhood years in Honduras at another production division, where his father had worked as a research scientist. His background was clearly rooted in the neocolonial history of the company, so much so that Robert had not become highly fluent in Spanish, though he had resided in Latin America for much of his life. Robert had attended boarding school in Europe and was educated as a military officer. He found that the military was not a suitable career for him. His father then arranged for him and his brother to work for the company. Robert had worked in many different locations, including Punta Blanca, before his promotion to the general manager's slot in Palo Amarillo. Jim had seen that Robert was very effective during crises, perhaps in part due to his military background. His subordinates admiringly described Robert with the English word *pusher*, meaning one who gets things done. Given his style of pushing to get results, Robert was eager to implement the different projects he envisioned, some of which could be done through TQM.

Robert was deeply concerned for the welfare of his employees, which was consistent with the paternalistic background of the company. On several occasions, Jim had conflicted with Robert over such company services as the commissary. As a reflection of the corporate cost-reduction emphasis, Jim had suggested that the commissary be spun off as a cooperative and weaned away from the company. Robert had vigorously objected, stating that the local merchant would begin charging too much without the company store to hold down prices.

Robert was strongly socialized to the company-town culture found in the production divisions. He spent most of his free time with company employees or contractors. In contrast, Julian attempted to develop social contacts outside the company. Though very capable and intellectually gifted, Robert's insularity made him somewhat resistant to change. He continued to exhibit the strong command-and-control orientation of the traditional general manager of the Tropical Export Company, even though he seemed to understand the basic tenets of TQM.

Palo Amarillo

Jim enjoyed the flight over the mountain range. Since there was only one pilot, he sometimes got a bit worried about the pilot's health. However, he sat up front with the pilot and chatted on the way. The pilot flew close to a dormant volcano, so that Jim could get a good view. They also noted that the landscape had changed after the earthquake. In poetic Latino speech, the pilot observed, "Look at how the accompanying landslides tore away the green cover, and exposed the raw earth. Then vegetation and the bleeding earth partially clogged the river arteries."

Upon arrival, Jim entered the company office and greeted the secretary. She said, "Don Robert had to go to the wharf to intervene in a labor conflict. He said that you should go to the guesthouse and that he would see you this evening at the club."

Jim went to the guesthouse, named after the general manager, who had once lived there. He was tired and decided to simply take it easy: eat lunch, nap, and go for a swim at the pool. Later, after dinner, he walked to the club.

In years past, Jim had been entertained by stories from people reminiscing about the neocolonial era. One time, a local Spanish businessman told Jim, "Many years ago, I bought the first car owned by a 'civilian' (i.e., noncompany resident) in Palo Amarillo. When it was delivered on the company train, the general manager initially refused to allow it to be unloaded, saying he hadn't given his authorization." Those listening all laughed at this story they had heard many times. Laughing at such command-and-control behavior of the managers was a way to deal with the submission subordinates felt in such a hierarchy. This command-and-control attitude had not changed over the years, though managers had perhaps become less direct in their assertion of control. In a sense, TQM allowed the same type of control but with a gentler face.

Another individual listening in added, "You know how I learned English; my boss said, 'No Spanish'!" Again they guffawed.

Such tales from the past were part of the folklore that made the company what it was. However, Jim had also seen the more raw side during his tenure as the HR manager. Jim recalled how for one department head hierarchy was more than simple power associated with a senior position. He had actually asked Jim to do a survey feedback of his department to find out if his subordinates held a sufficient degree of fear of him as the department manager.

Finally, Robert arrived. They greeted one another, and chatted for a few hours over a few beers. During the course of the conversation, they spoke of many things, including business.

Perhaps to taunt Jim, Robert said, "You know the TQM council has become a manager's council. I chose to limit membership to department heads. I want people who understand the way things work around here. Besides, your emphasis on participation might not be appropriate here. You know that if I even ask a question, they are trying to guess what's on my mind. The exception was one young supervisor who was challenging me too much, so I rotated him off the council."

Jim and Robert continued speaking, watching the last quarter of a play-off game on television. Robert left when the game ended.

Francisco

Jim remained at the bar. He didn't have to leave until noon the following day and had finished his business. He then noticed the entry of the former TQM coordinator from Punta Blanca, Francisco. Jim exclaimed, "Francisco, how are you? Do you work here now?"

They shook hands vigorously. "Nice to see you, Jim. Yes, I'm here now. Two years in a staff position was enough for me. It was an interesting experience but I'd rather be a boss. I'm now the purchasing manager here."

Jim thought this was an ideal opportunity to continue gathering information about TQM. They ordered coffee and sat down at a nearby table. Jim began, "While I was in Punta Blanca, Julian forced the quality council members to sit in a room with Jose, the production manager and second-in-command, until they could get it together to participate." They both laughed at the irony.

Francisco responded, "I can see how that would work, though I suspect you are puzzled."

Jim responded, "Well, yes, I am puzzled."

Francisco countered teasingly, "You think about it, and give me a call."

Jim smiled, "Okay, so you'll enlighten me later. How about telling me about your experiences with TQM?"

Francisco responded with a lengthy monologue, filled with the trials of any staff person attempting to facilitate change in a strong command-and-control organizational culture. This seemed a warm-up to his explanation of the success of cross-functional teams. Francisco continued, "After encountering initial resistance from the turf-conscious department heads, Julian told me not to push cross-functional problem solving quite so aggressively. Instead, he suggested limiting the problem-solving teams to intradepartmental teams until the department heads became more accepting. Later, Julian instructed me to get the department heads to agree on a respected operations manager, who would lead the team attacking the quality problem. The team leader was then empowered to choose the members of his or her team, which included people from other departments. The team leader chose people he respected, and with whom he had worked and had developed a sense of mutual respect and loyalty. These people met and analyzed the specific problem. Significant improvements in quality outcomes resulted. The market feedback has been very positive. By the way, how did the survey turn out?"

Jim had conducted an attitude survey contrasting TQM participants with nonparticipants in both Punta Blanca and Palo Amarillo. Jim responded, "It went well. Thanks for your help. Basically, the TQM participants in Punta Blanca had a more favorable set of attitudes than the nonparticipants. This was not true in Palo Amarillo in that there were no significant differences between the two groups. But I'm not sure why. What do you think?"

Francisco thought of responding but decided it best to avoid commentary on his superiors' actions.

The time was then very late. Both were tired and decided to call it a night. The next day Jim returned to the capital, to catch a flight to the United States.

48

Negotiating Work Hours

by Loren Falkenberg, University of Calgary, and
D. Ronald Franklin, executive in residence, University of Calgary

Part 1

The following case is designed to highlight the importance of effective communications when negotiating, particularly when the interests of the parties appear to diverge sharply. The principles involved apply to any form of negotiation; however, this case is based on a collective bargaining situation that actually occurred at a Canadian university some years ago.

Background

The university is required by law to negotiate wages and terms and conditions of employment with the bargaining agent (union) representing the support staff. The bargaining agent involved is a provincial union that negotiates for groups of employees in various public service areas—health care, postsecondary education, government services, and boards and agencies. The university local of the union represents a broad cross section of employees including clerical and secretarial staff, technicians, data processing personnel, library staff, food service, housing, and grounds and maintenance workers (including tradesmen, laborers, caretaking, and security staff).

The union negotiates a separate collective agreement for each of the employers with which it bargains. However, it has attempted to bring about a fairly high degree of standardization in the provisions relating to terms of employment and working conditions within its various collective agreements. On some major issues, the National Federation of Public Service union has developed "model clauses," which it recommends to the unions affiliated with it.

The 1995 round of bargaining is about to begin.

Management Position

The senior management negotiator, Susan Graves, has just been handed the union's proposals for a new collective agreement. She reads through them quickly and her heart sinks at the sight of such unreasonable demands. She sighs as she reads the proposed wording of a "new hours of work" clause. This is the fourth round of bargaining during which the union has proposed adding the following provision to the collective agreement:

"Regular hours of work for all employees shall consist of 40 hours per week performed between 8:00 a.m. and 4:30 p.m., Monday to Friday. Work performed outside these hours shall be compensated at double the regular rate of pay."

What is wrong with the union leaders? Why can't they get it through their heads that the university is open 24 hours a day, seven days per week for 52 weeks a year? Acceptance of the proposed hours of work clause would mean that everyone—including cleaning staff, residence workers, security officers, library staff, and everyone else who works shifts or weekends would receive overtime instead of straight time for regular hours of work. Such a provision might be acceptable in an organization made up entirely of office staff whose hours of work can conform with those proposed; however, it is simply not workable at a university.

Susan notices that the wording of the proposal is almost identical to the model clause that the National Federation was encouraging its members to negotiate. In addition, it is very similar to clauses contained in the collective agreements negotiated by the same union on behalf of five other locals—locals representing the office employees in organizations that did not have a need for shift or weekend work on a regular basis. Susan is certain that the union wants the same provision in all of its contracts regardless of its appropriateness in any given organization. She is determined that she is going to settle this issue permanently this year—and without making any further costly concessions!

Union Position

In preparation for the 1992 round of collective bargaining, George Lewis, the union business agent, held a series of meetings across the campus with the members of the university local to determine what changes were required in the collective agreement. One of those meetings was particularly stormy. It was a meeting with the staff members of the maintenance department—a department that was noted for its militant union attitude. The discussion that night centered around a contentious issue related to overtime pay for weekend work.

It had been the practice of the university each year to perform major electrical maintenance work during the month of May. Most of the work was performed on weekends to avoid disruption to scheduled classroom activities. The electricians worked their regular hours during the week and then performed the weekend work at overtime rates. However, in 1991, that practice was changed without warning. For the month of May only, the regular work schedules of the electricians had been changed from 40 hours performed on weekdays (Monday to Friday) to one in which straight time rates were paid for 40 hours of work scheduled from Wednesday through Sunday. This meant that the electricians had Mondays and Tuesdays off but had to work on the weekends without overtime compensation.

George Lewis and the local union officers were concerned. By changing the regular schedule during the month of May, management had found a way to avoid paying overtime for work performed on weekends. A closer look at the collective agreement revealed the fact that there was virtually no limitation on management's right to schedule regular work on weekends or, for that matter, on evening and night shifts. This meant that employees of the university had no assurance that their normal hours of work would not be changed at the whim of management.

In an attempt to correct the situation, the union decided to demand a change in the collective agreement that would protect all employees from such arbitrary and unfair actions on the part of management. The officers looked at the National Federation's "model clause" and the hours of work provisions that a number of other locals in the same union had successfully negotiated. As a result, when collective bargaining commenced in 1992, they tabled the hours of work proposal that Susan Graves found so offensive. Certainly, the proposal was not received with any enthusiasm. After the usual give, and take, of collective bargaining, some gains were made with the penalty rates for overtime, but management retained the right to reschedule shifts. The identical proposal was made in 1993 and again in 1994. In 1993, management offered to implement a schedule of premiums, which would be paid to anyone working shifts or weekends, and to increase the rate paid for overtime from time and a half to double time for all overtime hours worked on Saturdays and Sundays. Although the concession did not give the union the protection it wanted, it did represent a major monetary gain and would provide a precedent for other employers in the provincial public sector to follow. In 1994, the union was no more successful than in the previous year, but it did obtain a concession from management in the form of a provision requiring that the employer give a minimum of two weeks' notice of any change in the regular shift of an employee.

The electricians are still unhappy because they continue to work weekends at straight time rates during the month of May and, from the union's point of view, no real progress has been made to protect its members from unreasonable shift changes. The local union officers are both frustrated and determined that the situation must be corrected this year. Once again they have submitted a proposal to management containing the model clause that they first proposed in 1992.

George Lewis is not optimistic that he can convince management to accept the union's position, but he knows that something must be done to satisfy the local union officers.

Discussion Questions for Part 1

1. What are Susan's assumptions as she enters the negotiations?
2. What are the union's assumptions as it enters negotiations?
3. How do these assumptions influence their behaviors during negotiations?
4. What are the interests underlying the union's proposal (i.e., why is the union putting this proposal on the table)? What are the university's interests?

Negotiating Work Hours (Part 2)

The Bargaining Begins

Determined to resolve this contentious issue early in the current round of bargaining, Susan leads off by directing the union's attention to the hours of work proposal.

Susan: I can't understand why you persist in this same demand year after year. What's the matter with you people—don't you have any common sense at all?

George: We wouldn't have to ask for the same thing if you had any feelings for the working people. *You* don't have to work shifts or weekends. Why can't you see that we are only asking for a little consideration so our people can have some quality time with their families? We are only asking for the same rights that our members in other locals have. Why can't *you* treat the staff decently?

Susan: If we accepted your demand, we would have to contract out most of our support services to get the work done. Then your people would have lots of time to spend with their families! Is that what you want?

George: Look—we aren't here to listen to your threats about contracting out! We simply want fair working conditions for our members and we're willing to consider "job action" to get them! We're not prepared to discuss any other matter until we get this one settled. We're going to give you a couple of hours to think this over. It's 2 o'clock now—we'll be back at 4:00 P.M. When we return, you had better be prepared to show us that you want to resolve this thing without a strike!

Susan: Now who is making the threats? I'd suggest that you and your team think seriously about what you just said because I can assure you that we have no intention of accepting your proposal.

The negotiating teams break to discuss their positions. Both George and Susan realize that they are further away now from resolving this matter than they were when they started the discussion. The next session will have to be different.

When the parties return to the bargaining table after the break, the union opens the discussion.

George: Well, I hope that you've had enough time to reconsider your position.

Susan: Your proposal is still not acceptable. Are you prepared to withdraw it?

George: No—but our team would like to hear your explanation for rejecting it.

Susan: I should think the reasons would be obvious. How do you expect the university to function if we have to pay overtime for all hours worked by staff scheduled to work on afternoon, evening, and weekend shifts?

George: Overtime pay is only fair compensation for working undesirable hours. Other employers seem to manage—why can't the university?

Susan: Well, our needs are different. We operate 24 hours a day and 7 days a week. The other employers with whom you have negotiated this clause all conduct business only during regular office hours. Why aren't you satisfied with the concessions we've already made in the areas of overtime and weekend premiums? Surely you don't expect more?

George: Why are you unwilling to give our people decent working conditions?

Susan: We've been having this argument for four years now. You know we can't accept your proposal.

George: And you know that we can't go back to the membership without a solution to the problem.

Susan: Well, tell me, again, what your problem is. I mean, why do you believe such a restrictive clause is necessary?

George: You know why. Your managers don't know how to treat people fairly.

Susan: I don't agree with that statement. Our managers really do care. And I believe that we can solve the problem if we can identify it.

George: Maybe. But don't think that we're going to give up our demand for fair treatment.

Susan: I'm not sure that we're making much progress. Let's break for the day and meet again at 10:00 A.M. tomorrow.

George: Okay. But, when you come back tomorrow, be prepared to make some real concessions on this issue.

Susan is relieved that she was able to end the bargaining session without any further deterioration in the relationship with the union. She and the members of her bargaining team meet briefly to discuss the situation. They share their feelings of frustration and disappointment. Susan knows that she must find a mutually satisfactory solution to the problem. She has also come to realize that traditional distributive bargaining techniques are not likely to break the impasse on this issue. During the meeting, the management team decides that it must take a fresh look at the union's position on this matter. A strategy is decided upon that everyone hopes will redefine the problem and uncover new solutions.

George and his team also leave the bargaining table unhappy and somewhat bitter that management is so insensitive to their needs. George knows that his bargaining committee expects him to come up with something to protect employees from what appears to be the arbitrary and capricious shift changes made by management. However, he also recognizes that he has been unable to make any headway on this issue so far. George decides that it is time to reassess their proposal to ensure that they are demanding what they really need.

Discussion Questions for Part 2

1. Why did the negotiators fail to exchange any information?
2. What specific communication mistakes were made by the negotiators? Provide examples.
3. When are breaks effective in a negotiation? Comment on the use of breaks in this negotiation.
4. What needs to be done to get the negotiations back on track?

Negotiating Work Hours (Part 3)

It is 10:00 A.M. the following morning and the union negotiating team arrives at the meeting room. Susan offers George a cup of coffee. They sit down and begin negotiations again.

Susan: What incident or issue made your members believe that they needed a restrictive hours of work clause to protect them?

George: I'm sure that there were many, but the one in the electrical maintenance department was the worst.

Susan: Let's focus on the maintenance department. What happened?

George: Your foreman screwed our people when he changed the crew's shift schedule so that they had to work on Saturdays and Sundays at straight time.

Susan: I don't think I understand. Was the schedule changed on a permanent basis?

George: No, only during the month of May. The same thing has happened each year since then, even though we've tried to get things changed each year at the bargaining table, but you don't want to listen to us.

Susan: I'm listening now. Why are the shifts changed each year?

George: To complete the annual electrical maintenance schedule. Things are quiet on the weekends in May, so that is the best time to do the work.

Susan: Then am I correct in assuming that you don't disagree with the need to get the work done on weekends in May?

George: We don't disagree with that, but by changing shifts you cut our members off overtime and make them work at straight time rates on the weekends. That means you can change anyone's schedule to meet your needs and to avoid paying the overtime we won through collective bargaining. You are abusing your rights!

Susan: Whoa there! Let's see if we can find a solution to this problem. Before we started changing the shift schedule, weren't your members working seven full shifts a week for four weeks straight? Weren't they tired?

George: Yes, they were tired, but it was only for a month.

Susan: Are you saying that the crew members preferred the seven-day shifts?

George: Yes, that's what I'm saying. But you guys were too cheap to pay the overtime.

Susan: It wasn't just a matter of money. We were also concerned about the strain on the crew members.

George: I don't believe you.

Susan: Let's get back to the problem. Why did the crew prefer the longer working hours?

George: Because of the overtime. Some of them took the overtime compensation in the form of additional pay, which helped them finance their vacations in the summer months. Others took the compensation as time off so that they could have longer vacations with their families.

Susan: Do you have any other specific examples of temporary shift changes to avoid paying overtime?

George: No, but that doesn't mean that you wouldn't do it if you wanted to save money. That's why we have to change the collective agreement.

Susan: We've had the same hours of work provisions for nearly 15 years and I'm not aware of any other cases like this. Are you?

George: No, but I have to have something to take back to my membership. You know the problem—how would you propose to solve it?

Susan: I'd suggest that we leave the agreement the way it is and the university will guarantee that it will no longer make seasonal changes in the electrical crew's schedule. In addition, during the life of the agreement, we will discuss all temporary shift changes with you before they go into effect. Together, we will have solved your problem and the university will be able to maintain its evening and weekend shifts at a reasonable cost. Okay?

George: I'm not sure. Let's see if I have this straight. You're saying that if we drop our hours-of-work proposal, you'll promise to not change the electrical maintenance crew's shift schedule for the month of May each year?

Susan: Right!

George: And they will be paid for the weekend work at the overtime rates, just like the collective agreement says?

Susan: Right again!

George: But what happens if you decide to change some other crew's schedule just to avoid paying overtime?

Susan: It won't happen! I've told you—we will discuss all temporary changes in shift schedules with you before they are implemented for the life of the agreement.

George: Are we just supposed to accept your word on this? Do you expect us to "fly on faith"? We need some protection in the agreement.

Susan: We've always kept our word. We've never let you down before. George, we could spend weeks trying to come up with some wording that would satisfy both of us or we can agree to our proposal and get on with other matters.

George: I hear you, but I need time to talk to the other members of my committee.

Susan: Okay. Will 15 minutes be enough time?

George: I think so.

Thirty minutes pass and George and his committee finally return to the bargaining table. They all look somber and it's hard to know what their answer will be.

George: We talked about your proposal. I can't say that we're very happy about it, but we want to move on to talk about a new dental plan. If you keep your word, then our problem on shift changes has been solved.

Susan: Then, it's a deal?

George: It's a deal, but we'll be back if it doesn't work.

Discussion Questions for Part 3

1. Why did this interaction produce a better outcome? What were the turning points?
2. How did the initial assumptions of the negotiators impact the exchange of information in the first session? How did they affect the exchange of information in the second session?
3. Identify the elements of positive communication in this discussion.
4. Which questions were the most effective? Why?

Preferential Treatment?

by Brian Park

On a dreary morning in May 1995, Paul found himself sitting on the floor of the hallway, crouched against the cold wall, feeling dejected and desperate. The bustling cacophony of the people in nearby offices seemed distant and surreal to him. Immobilized by his shock, Paul just sat there looking down at the floor. He wanted to rationalize the situation in an attempt to contain his despair, but so many thoughts were going through his mind that he soon became confused and unable to think clearly.

Paul

Paul was a junior at the Upland University and was finishing the last quarter of his third year. Paul was in his early twenties. He was Korean American; he had been born in Korea and had come to the United States when he was nine years old. He began his academic career as a biochemistry major, intending to become a doctor, but, having failed his organic chemistry series twice, he had to drop out of biochemistry and change his major in the middle of his sophomore year.

Paul was not only having problems with organic chemistry, he was also struggling with many other classes in the biochemistry major. Paul was stuck in a cycle; the more poorly he performed in his classes, the harder it was to remain motivated to try. His dream of becoming a doctor was certainly slipping away. The problems compounded until he was placed on academic probation, and consequently, utterly crushed by his failure, he decided to take a leave of absence to clear his thoughts and reassess his career goals.

During the year that Paul took off from school, he struggled to accept his shortcomings, but this was not easy. The thoughts of his failure haunted him every day and hampered his courage to continue with his educational career because he was afraid that he would fail again. Ultimately, he decided to finish what he had begun, and he returned to school.

When Paul returned to school, his grade point average was 2.7. At this point, he was very discouraged. However, he found when he changed his major to psychology, he performed well in the courses, and the subjects were much more to his liking. Paul received almost all A's after he changed his major and had brought up his G.P.A. to 3.6. He was very excited about his newly found interest in psychology and wanted to pursue, to a deeper extent, social psychology.

Paul was assigned, just as other students had been, one academic advisor since his freshman year. From the very beginning, he sought Dr. Richard David's counsel, especially when he was having difficulty with his biochemistry major.

Dr. Richard David

Dr. David had been working for the Upland University as a principal academic advisor. He had a Ph.D. and, in addition to being an academic advisor, he was also a professor at the university. Dr. David was an unmarried Caucasian man in his mid-forties. He had known Paul since his freshman year, and had met with him six times prior to the meeting in question.

The first couple of meetings Paul had with Dr. David were standard introductory consultation sessions. Dr. David was the consultant for each student's schedule and registration. Dr. David's first encounter with Paul was nothing more than standard and took less than 5 minutes. He asked if Paul had any difficulty choosing classes for his first quarter and, when Paul responded that he hadn't, the meeting was over.

The third and fourth meetings consisted of Dr. David consulting Paul about his difficulty with the organic chemistry series. Paul was required by the school to speak with his advisor regarding his academic standing. Unfortunately, there was no substantial advice given, except that Paul needed to pass his organic chemistry classes in order to remain in the major. The conversation was professional and distant.

The last two meetings involved Paul's change of major from biochemistry to psychology. The main reason for these meetings was to obtain consent from the academic advisor, and to confirm schedule changes for the following quarters. These meetings were still very formal. Nothing much was said between Dr. David and Paul. They were brief and to the point.

Paul's Meeting with Dr. David

Paul had met with Dr. David earlier that afternoon, seeking academic counseling and information regarding his career options. Paul entered the office, and Dr. David motioned for him to sit down. Paul chose a seat located to the right of Dr. David's desk. He was typing something, and the silence that permeated the room made the clicking of the keyboard seemed loud. After what felt like five minutes of silence and clicking, Dr. David finished typing. He asked in a loud and resounding voice, "So Paul, what do we need to talk about?" Paul was momentarily stunned by the loud coldness of Dr. David's voice, and paused to wonder what he could say to ease the tension. Feeling intimidated, Paul brought up the reason he had come into Dr. David's office. "I am a bit confused about what I want to do after I graduate, and I wanted to talk to you to find out if you could give me some ideas about what's out there."

Dr. David said nothing as he turned his chair around again to face his computer. Paul was feeling ignored, but soon realized that Dr. David was trying to bring up his student records. He asked, "What is your social security number?" After he got the number from Paul and punched it into the computer, he sat there looking at Paul's records, shaking his head from time to time, his eyebrows crunching to the center of his forehead, making a prominent wrinkle. He was tapping his long fingers on the table. Paul felt uncomfortable, as if he had come into an interview and was being judged, as if the computer screen had exposed something horrible to its viewer.

Silence fell over the room again. At this point, Dr. David turned his chair to face Paul and asked, "What would you like to do with yourself, I mean, after you graduate?" Paul thought, "That's what I just asked you," but did not verbalize this thought. Paul still felt very intimidated by Dr. David's loud voice, the way he accentuated every syllable with his lips, the way he sat in his chair with his arms and legs crossed, and how he looked at Paul without blinking. However, Paul's frustration overcame his intimidation, and he told Dr. David about his interest to study further in graduate school.

Dr. David looked at Paul condescendingly; his eyes seemed to become bigger, as if he was surprised. He untangled his arms from his chest and moved them to the back of his head, and for a moment, Paul saw a very awkward, one-sided smirk on his face. Dr. David asked Paul where he would possibly like to go and for what. "Well, I have an interest in psychology, and I would like to pursue that field further, possibly social psychology. I was hoping to go to school somewhere in southern California." Dr. David looked at his watch, and didn't seem to have heard what Paul had said. He finally looked at Paul and said, "Well, then that's what you should do. Did you have anything else to ask me?" Paul felt outraged, but said nothing more. "Who am I kidding?" Paul silently asked himself, "I'm not getting anywhere with this guy."

After he had finished his consultation and left the office, he realized that he had forgotten his cap, so he returned to retrieve it. Dr. David was consulting another student, so Paul decided to wait outside in the hallway until the consultation was finished.

His door was open, but probably neither Dr. David nor the student realized that Paul was outside waiting. Paul did not want to disturb them, so he sat quietly outside. He could hear their conversation clearly, and could not help but listen to the exchange between Dr. David and the student. The consultation had just started, and Dr. David asked the female student, "What can I help you with today?" She paused for a moment and answered, "I am thinking about going to graduate school, and I hope that you can help me consider my options."

Dr. David was very talkative. The young woman had very little to say, except for occasional "yes's" and "no's." Dr. David talked almost incessantly, while he shared with her the various fields she could pursue, and potential careers available after graduate school. He told her about the different schools available, academic programs, and campus life. He also shared with her his personal experience as a student on one of those campuses.

Comparing his earlier conversation with Dr. David and the conversation unfolding before him, Paul was confused. He could not verbalize his thoughts and emotions, but he knew he had been treated differently and was ultimately wronged.

After the consultation of over 30 minutes, the student apparently stood up to leave. As she was leaving, Dr. David said, "If you feel that you need more assistance, and I can help you further, you can call me at home. Here's my number," and the meeting was finally over.

When the student walked out of Dr. David's office, Paul recognized her. They were both juniors, and she was majoring in psychology as well. As a transfer student from a junior college in northern California, she was finishing up her first year and a half at the university. She was Caucasian, in her early twenties.

Feeling that he had been discriminated against, Paul walked into Dr. David's office. He wanted to confront the advisor, but felt unable to do so. Paul awkwardly grabbed his hat and left. Realizing what just took place, Dr. David looked shocked and almost embarrassed, but hesitated to say anything.

What to Do?

The next day, Paul tried to think of the best way to deal with his strange predicament. He was more than disturbed. Paul had never been exposed to such an overt, yet subtle, act of discrimination. Without even trying, Paul's mind kept playing the scene over and over again. He was hurt, and he didn't want to see Dr. David ever again, least of all as his academic advisor. He wondered what his next steps should be.

Reputation in Jeopardy

by Amber Borden

Amber Borden, special events planner for Home Savings of America, felt her stomach knot as her coworker, Beth, told her about some remarks made about her by a manager in another department. Although Amber took it all in very quietly, inside she was in turmoil. She couldn't believe how a little lie could place her reputation in such jeopardy. After all, she had only been following her boss's orders.

Amber's boss, Sarah Davis, vice president of corporate meetings and events, had been with Home Savings for over 11 years. She was approximately 33 years old and had been planning events for the company for the majority of her employment, moving quickly from a secretary to a vice president due to her obvious skill. Amber enjoyed Sarah's excellent sense of humor, quick wit, and how adept she was at handling potential conflict with extraordinary finesse. On the other hand, Sarah had little patience for ignorance or laziness or those who did not put their best effort forward. Amber knew that Sarah and most of the other employees at Home Savings of America had been under a lot of stress lately.

Home Savings of America

Home Savings of America provided checking and savings services along with various types of consumer loans. It employed 10,000 people, most of whom worked at savings branch and loan offices located throughout the United States. Amber, age 25, worked at the corporate headquarters in Irwindale, California. In her six years with Home Savings, she had worked in various departments such as Customer Service, Residential Lending, Real Estate Owned (REO), Internal Audit, and the Executive Department. Through these various positions, she obtained broad knowledge of the organization's culture and overall objectives. She transferred to the Meetings and Events Department in October 1997, where she was learning the processes and procedures of event planning, and how to organize and prioritize projects.

Amber had an excellent reputation at the corporate headquarters. She was extremely professional, articulate, intelligent, meticulously dressed, and fit the image that Home Savings desired of its professionals. She enjoyed her work at the company—especially the feeling that she was working for a company that cared. In fact, the company mission statement was W.E. C.A.R.E., which was an acronym for six values and a set of behaviors that many employees at every level embraced and reflected how Amber tried to conduct herself at work. (See Exhibit 1.)

As a long-standing institution, the culture and values were deeply embedded in the company's operations. While, on the one hand, it was a somewhat conservative, old-fashioned company that provided and enforced strict management policies and procedures, it was also a company where the CEO had an open door, and many employees participated and enjoyed teamwork. Members of departments worked hard to support the branches and other departments in the company in a responsive, professional way.

Changing Times

Yet times were changing. After 108 years in operation, the company was being merged with Washington Mutual, and its Irwindale, California, headquarters was being shut down. Amber and most of the employees at corporate headquarters felt hurt that their loyalty and dedication to the company had come to naught. The W.E. C.A.R.E. philosophy appeared to be just a piece of paper, and people felt that they had been betrayed.

One of the many times Home Savings upper management solicited employees to unite and exercise those W.E. C.A.R.E values was a few months prior to the announcement of the merger with Washington Mutual. Home Savings CEO, Charlie Rinehart, addressed his workforce and asked for their support. Home Savings had developed a proposal to attempt a hostile takeover of another large financial institution, Great Western. (A hostile takeover is when Home Savings attempts to buy enough shares of Great Western to own it, even though Great Western didn't want to be purchased by Home Savings.) Great Western was opposed to the takeover and went looking for a "white knight" to save them from their fate. Great Western found their white knight in Washington Mutual and began proceedings to enter into a friendly merger with them. That's when the war between Home Savings and Washington Mutual over Great Western began.

Employees put forth tremendous effort and many worked overtime to try to obtain the advantage over Washington Mutual. Home Savings employees even created a slogan and designed T-shirts that exemplified their emotional involvement in the battle. The T-shirts read "Great Western, phone Home," and were distributed to all line staff involved in the takeover effort. Even employees who were not directly involved in the battle became emotionally involved in the takeover effort.

In the end, Home Savings lost, and after all of its hard work, the disappointment was devastating to the company morale. However, employees who were not privy to the organization's strategic planning process had no idea how truly devastating it was. Without a merger big enough to make the company too large to acquire, Home Savings was a sitting duck for a hostile takeover. So, immediately following Home Savings loss of Great Western to Washington Mutual, Mr. Rinehart approached Washington Mutual offering to sell Home Savings.

Employees later learned that Mr. Rinehart knew that Washington Mutual would close the corporate facility, and felt all their efforts were rewarded by a trip to the unemployment office. Employees began saying that Mr. Rinehart had less than honorable intentions. They believed that they had done their best to attain the objectives of the company, which included attaining 15 percent return on equity (a financial measure that demonstrated good financial management) and cutting overhead expenses by 10 percent. After that, W.E. C.A.R.E. became something employees joked about. Employees began spending a lot of time talking, complaining, and blaming executive management. It only made matters worse when they found out that executive management was making several hundred million dollars in personal income from the sale of the company.

Too Busy to Help

Soon after the announcement that Home Savings would be taken over by Washington Mutual, Lydia Ulmass, department manager for Loan Sales Administration, called Amber's department to request copies of the last 10 years of videotapes of the annual recognition event given to top-producing loan officers. Lydia was roughly 55 years old and supported loan consultants for most of her approximate 20-year tenure at Home Savings. Lydia wanted to create a final farewell video for her loan consultants, so she requested the keys to the events department storeroom in order to get the videos herself. Amber's boss, Sarah, did not like anyone having access to the storeroom unchaperoned, as many sample and excess gift items, props, and company logoed giveaways were kept there. Therefore, she volunteered Amber and Beth, Amber's coworker who had worked with Home Savings for 15 years, to find the tapes for Lydia.

Amber and Beth went to the storage room and searched through several boxes to find the prior years' tapes. They located them and brought them back to their boss. Sarah then asked Amber to call Lydia to let her know she could come and pick them up.

When Amber called, she got Lydia's voice mail. "Hi, Lydia, this is Amber. We've retrieved the tapes that you needed. You can come and pick them up any time. I'll be in and out of my office, but I'll leave them on my desk for you."

When Amber returned, she listened to a voice message from Lydia. "Hi Amber, this is Lydia. I'm without an administrative assistant today, and I'm really shorthanded due to the merger. Would you mind bringing the tapes over for me? Thanks a lot."

Amber didn't mind at all; taking the videos to Lydia was an insignificant favor for a manager whom she had a lot of contact with and had gotten along with over the past years. Lydia and Amber were located at opposite ends of the same building on the same floor. It was approximately a two-minute walk.

Amber got up to take the tapes to Lydia and told Sarah that she was going to deliver them. Sarah became upset and directed Amber not to deliver the tapes.

"Call her back and tell her the events department is too busy to bring them over today, and ask if they could be sent by interoffice mail." Sarah looked over at Beth and then back at Amber, "We just saved Lydia a lot of time because she didn't have to go down to the storeroom to find those tapes. The least she could do is come and pick up the videos."

Amber accepted Sarah's authority in the situation and did as she was directed even though she was uncomfortable lying to Lydia. Lydia had always had a good opinion of Amber and they had heretofore worked together without incident.

When Lydia received the voice message from Amber, she got upset and forwarded Amber's message to Sarah with a message of her own. "Sarah, Amber left this message on my voice mail. Would you do me a favor and ask her to please deliver the tapes to me? I really need them and I'm swamped. Thanks."

Sarah told Amber about the message and said, "I'm just going to act like I never received it."

The following day, Amber left for an out-of-town conference. While checking her messages later that day she discovered another message from Lydia stating that she was really disappointed that Amber could not "find it in her heart to deliver them," and that she would try to come over and get them herself. Her tone indicated to Amber that she did not believe Amber was too busy and assumed that she was being lazy or uncooperative. Sarah was attending the conference, too, so Amber told her what Lydia had said.

"Don't worry about it, Amber," Sarah said. "There is nothing you can do now, anyway, since we're not in the office."

A few days later Lydia ran into Beth, and Lydia proceeded to make derogatory comments about Amber. Beth already knew the story and knew that Amber was getting blamed for something she had no control over. She also knew that Sarah did not have any intention of correcting the problem, but Beth was also unable to tell Lydia the truth without blaming Sarah in the process. Beth, who was very nonconfrontational, avoided becoming involved in the conflict by telling Lydia that Amber really had been too busy.

About a week later a gentleman called on Sarah's line. When Amber answered it and then told her boss who was calling, Sarah told her to have the person call Lydia. A couple of days later, Lydia again made derogatory comments about Amber to Beth. Lydia told Beth that Amber passed off a call to her to handle when Amber could have handled it. Lydia was unaware that Amber had not asked what the person's issue was, she simply told Sarah who was calling, and then transferred the call as she was directed.

From Lydia's point of view, Amber was simply too uncooperative or too lazy to take care of the videos or the phone call. The issue then became even more inflamed when Lydia told Beth that Amber didn't like her because she hadn't hired her a few years ago. She assumed that was the reason Amber was being uncooperative. Approximately three years before this situation, Amber had discussed working for Lydia, but had never applied or interviewed for the position. She had worked with Lydia without incident since then, so it seemed odd to her that Lydia would choose that particular instance as the root cause of the problem.

What to Do?

Amber had an excellent reputation with Home Savings for the previous six years and was now in a situation where a manager could damage that reputation. She was not sure what measures to take to change this manager's assumptions about her. It seemed that in every instance where she and Lydia had come in contact, even indirectly, her actions were not given the benefit of the doubt. Amber did not want to implicate her own manager in an effort to exonerate herself because it would seem like she was trying to direct the blame to Sarah. However, if she did not tell Lydia the truth and made up another reason for her behavior, then she would simply be replacing one lie with another. Amber thought the truth might prompt Lydia to confront Sarah, shifting the problem between Amber and Lydia and creating one between Amber and Sarah. Amber liked that idea even less since Sarah was the one who had control over her reviews and merit increases. Amber hoped to stay on with the corporate headquarters as long as possible. There might even be an opportunity to get a job at Washington Mutual. She couldn't afford to have either Lydia or Sarah upset with her. Amber wondered what to do.

Exhibit 1

W.E. C.A.R.E.
Homes Savings of America
Work Together
- Openly share information and resources with others
- Put the team's needs above personal gain
- Listen to input from teammates to reach the best solution
- State your opinion but support team decisions

Exemplify Integrity
- Be open and honest with others
- Live up to commitments through actions
- Adhere to the highest ethical standards in dealing with others
- Be dedicated to the agreed upon direction of the company
- Praise in public, critique in private

Coach to Win
- Encourage professional growth through honest and timely feedback
- Provide appreciative feedback to others
- Actively seek feedback from others on how you can be more effective
- Create an environment where people feel appreciated and recognized
- Teach others the skills and techniques needed to do their jobs properly
- Help others to be and do their best

Act Now
- Demonstrate high energy and a "can do" attitude
- Foster a sense of urgency in others
- Be willing to do whatever it takes to help get the job done
- Persevere until the job is done and challenges are met

Reach to Improve
- Be proactive to change
- Always look for a better solution
- Be willing to change your point of view
- Support new ways to be creative

Empower Yourself
- Focus on finding solutions and achieving results rather than blaming others
- Accept responsibility for your mistakes and learn from them
- Accept responsibility for team decisions
- Empower others to take responsibility for their actions
- Be willing to take prudent risks to move the company forward

Richard Prichard and the Federal Triad Programs

by Earle Hall

Friday, January 9, 1998

8:55 A.M.

Richard entered the building where he worked, frustrated that he had to wake up from a deep sleep in his nice, soft, warm bed just to come to this place. "Well, at least it's warmer in here than the 28 degree weather outside," he thought. He walked down the long, empty hallway. The bright lights and the clacking sound of his shoe heels slapping against the off-white, freshly waxed, tiled floor gradually snapped him out of his daydream of driving back home and returning to bed. As usual, he was the first one in the office. As he walked the length of the hall, Richard checked the other office doors, hoping that maybe someone else was here for a change, which was wishful thinking on his part. The words, "Thank God it's Friday," repeatedly flashed in his mind like a neon sign as he started some coffee brewing in the copy room.

1:33 P.M.

After the phone calls to parents, receiving nonstop faxes from other colleges, typing memos, copying documents, meetings with students, filing student information, and performing many other tasks that seemed to never end, it was finally lunchtime. This was Richard's average day. The work just kept coming. As Richard passed the halfway mark of his workday, he noticed that Dr. Duncan, director of Washington-Hall University's Federal Programs, had just walked in.

5:45 P.M.

As Richard finished round two of his day, he happened to run into Dr. Duncan in the hallway. She stopped to talk with Richard, asking him how his day went. Richard told her how long, but productive, it was. She continued talking as Richard zoned in and out, thinking about enjoying another weekend. After working 50-plus hours every week, the weekends were his time to regroup and do things for himself.

He was immediately yanked back into the real world as the words fell from Dr. Duncan's lips, "Can you come into the office tomorrow afternoon to help me with a grant at about 1:00?"

There was a long pause, but Richard managed to say, "I don't know. I may have some other things to take care of." He knew very well that he had no other plans but to enjoy his weekend of relaxation. He needed to regain the sanity that he always managed to lose when at work in the office.

She then asked, as nonchalant as when she asked the first question, "Well, how about Sunday?" It was obvious to him that she wanted any morsel of time and effort that she could possibly squeeze from him, even though he worked so hard for her and the program during the week. Richard was always the first one in and the last one to go home. He never received any overtime pay, and he was not offered any bonus pay for participation in the extra weekend project either.

He stood thinking, "The nerve of this woman to ask me to come in on a weekend! I know that there are other people who are more qualified, and more important, who don't do as much work during the week." All he could feel was anger.

She noticed that he looked a bit perturbed, and, in an attempt to give him some encouragement, informed him that her daughter would be coming in to help and so would Stephen, one of Richard's coworkers. Richard thought, with a great deal of sarcasm, "Oh, she's too kind."

The Organization

The program he worked for, 100 percent federally funded, originally started with three separate programs, called Federal Programs. It was currently a group of about six programs designed to serve low-income populations that were underrepresented in higher education. The various programs focused on groups such as the following:

- First-generation college students from low-income backgrounds,
- students who were on or in danger of being placed on academic probation, and
- students who were physically disabled.

The services provided included tutoring and counseling.

The Staff

The employees involved with the program were Mr. Adams, Mr. Butler, Ms. Sutton, and Richard. Mr. Adams was the tutorial coordinator/counselor and had been at Washington-Hall since the inception of the grant in the autumn of 1997. He was an African American male in his late forties. As stated in the grant, he was responsible for coordinating all events pertaining to the students' academics, such as general and private tutoring sessions, study habit seminars, and so on. However, he always managed to get involved in activities that took away time that was allotted to work on his projects pertaining to the program. He was very high-strung. Coworkers were constantly complaining about his lack of interpersonal skills and short temper. Mr. Adams had worked as a teacher and had also served as a part-time counselor for one of the other programs during the summer. Based on his knowledge and his experience with the programs, he was able to secure the full-time coordinator/counselor position for the Federal Program.

Mr. Butler was the counseling coordinator/counselor and joined the program staff from another institution of higher learning in the winter of 1998. He was also an African American male in his late forties. He was responsible for the students' mental well-being. That included scheduling regular counseling sessions with students and planning retreats or other seminars that dealt with the students' mental well-being while in school. Mr. Butler was much more sociable than Mr. Adams, but there was no "in-between" point with his temper. Either he was in a good mood and very understanding, jovial, and inviting, or he was in a bad mood and quickly became very impatient and irritable.

Ms. Sutton, an African American female in her mid-thirties, was the head coordinator/counselor for the program. She had worked with other programs for several years, but the winter of 1998 was her first year working with this particular program. Her position was not originally in the grant but became necessary when the personalities of Mr. Adams and Mr. Butler conflicted, and this conflict interfered with the program objectives. Dr. Duncan developed the duties of this position, which primarily included supervising the staff and counseling students. Ms. Sutton was an easygoing person who liked to get results. She would not hesitate to let the staff know when deadlines were approaching and assigned tasks to achieve the objectives.

Dr. Duncan, an African American female in her late forties, was the director of the Federal Programs at Washington-Hall University. As such, she also served as the director of the six individual federal programs at the institution, where Richard was assigned. She was the grant writer for all of the programs at the college and was the final authority on any matter concerning the programs at the university. Her requests superseded all others. She was not a micromanager. She was the kind of manager who allowed the program coordinators the autonomy necessary to do their jobs. She was not too concerned with when one came to work or when one left. But when she asked a staff member about deadlines, she wanted to hear that it was done, not that it was still being worked on. Failure to do so would cause her to take disciplinary action.

Richard, an African American male in his early twenties, was the executive assistant of the program. Along with Mr. Adams, he had been working with the program since the inception of the grant in the autumn of 1997. As stated in the grant, he was responsible for assisting in coordination of program-sponsored events. He also maintained student files, kept track of all interoffice documents, and performed all of the clerical duties of the program. Since Richard and Mr. Adams were the first two full-time staff members working solely for the program, the work was divided between the two of them. Mr. Adams would always direct Richard to where the needed information could be found. However, somewhere along the line, Richard was left alone to do the rest, because Mr. Adams did not contribute as much as expected. Mr. Adams delegated many responsibilities but rarely helped to carry out the necessary tasks. Because of this, many coordinator duties, such as program and activity planning, student selection for the program, and many other things, unofficially became Richard's responsibilities.

Washington-Hall University was Richard's alma mater. The school had an excellent reputation for producing African American male leaders for over a century. Richard took the values to heart, and they became part of his identity. While working with the program, he tried to exemplify qualities such as loyalty, integrity, and persistence in his work. His salary was a little bit more than half of what the coordinators were making. He did not mind this gap between the salaries when he was hired. He was shown the grant before he accepted the job, and his duties were clearly stated in the grant. In his opinion, the compensation was just.

All program coordinator/counselors were required to have at least a master's degree and experience in education or program coordination. The executive assistant was required to have at least a bachelor's degree as well as some clerical experience. All of the staff had the necessary credentials. Based on the qualifications stated in the grant, the know-how was supposed to come from the coordinators. The executive assistant's role was to keep things in order, which made the counselor/coordinators' jobs easier.

Two other relevant employees were Stephen and Dorothy. Stephen was a 24-year-old African American male. He was also an alumnus of Washington-Hall University. He worked as an executive assistant with a related program. He had been working for the program since the summer of 1997. His job was similar to Richard's. He assisted the program coordinators and mostly handled the clerical aspect of the program. His situation was also similar to Richard's, in that he received much more work than he was supposed to, due to the abuse of power in his program. Stephen was a loyal and persistent worker as well, but he knew that if he appeared to be busy, responsibilities would not be assigned to him as much. Therefore, they would be passed to another executive assistant, usually Richard. Stephen was successful in his efforts to be assigned as little work as possible. However, when he was told directly that he was to be responsible for a task, he did it to the best of his ability.

Dorothy, a 23-year-old African American female, was an undergraduate work-study student. She began working as a work-study student for the program in 1996. Work-study students were generally assigned to assist in the daily operation of the programs, doing things such as answering the phones, making copies, and other minor but important tasks. Since they were work-study students and not program specific, they generally rotated to wherever their assistance was needed. Her mother, Dr. Duncan, called on her when she needed assistance with other tasks.

The Problem

As time progressed since Richard's first day on the job, so did Richard's responsibilities, while his satisfaction rapidly decreased. His duties increased, due to his coworkers not fulfilling their own duties as described under their job titles in the grant. Coworkers began to continually come in late to work. Some coworkers engaged in activities on the job that were not work related. The coordinators, through the delegation of responsibilities, were abusing power. Richard received many demands during the day, many of which did not fall under his job description and were clearly under the coordinator positions. On some days, a few of Richard's coworkers would leave the office for the day, earlier than they were supposed to. This would leave Richard to do the work that was left behind. Richard could have left some of the work and complained that the work was coordinator work, but he felt that as a part of the team, it was his responsibility to make sure that whatever was assigned to the team was completed, no matter what. If the tasks were not carried out, that would mean failure for the team and for the program. He was concerned about what would happen to the students that the program served if these tasks were not performed. His loyalty forced him to take on the added responsibility voluntarily. This was why his workday never ended at 5:00 P.M., like everybody else's. He did raise the possibility to Dr. Duncan of being paid overtime. He let her know that not everyone on staff was doing their job, which placed a great deal of responsibility on him. The matter was always answered with, "I'll look into it and get back to you." The staff members at fault were reprimanded, but no effective changes were ever made.

Another problem was the perceived duties that came with each title. Some in the organization felt that this was a rigid bureaucracy and that orders came from the top down with no questions asked. In the coordinators' minds, this mentality justified the inequitable assignment of responsibilities. Some other coordinators were not sure what their duties were, even though they were clearly stated in the grant. Since there were three coordinators, and the grant only defined two coordinator positions, there was always conflict when coordinators felt that their boundaries had been crossed. Part of that was due to seniority in the organization. People with the most seniority felt that they were entitled to more say in the organization. In actuality, seniority did not play a part in authority in the organization.

The Decision

As Richard stood there thinking about how he should answer Dr. Duncan's request, questions about why she was asking him in particular and the consequences of his decision came to mind.

Do not read Part B until told to do so by your instructor.

Richard Prichard and the Federal Triad Programs (B)

The Decision

It did not seem that Dr. Duncan would accept a simple "no" for an answer, so Richard eventually gave in to her request. In addition to this, he figured that it would be a great deal of work. He hoped that by assisting with the task, he would make the load a bit lighter for the rest of the group. He agreed to arrive at 1:00 P.M. on Saturday, as she had requested. As Richard's Friday just turned into a Thursday, he left the office that evening feeling like it was Monday all over again.

The Deed

Richard drove into the parking lot that Saturday afternoon. He arrived at 1:00 P.M. on the dot, only to find that his was the only car in the parking lot. He figured that Dr. Duncan was probably just stuck in traffic or experiencing something beyond her control, but was definitely on her way. So he waited and waited. Finally Dr. Duncan and Dorothy showed up at 2:15 P.M. Richard was already mad that he had to give up a Saturday afternoon, but now he was even madder because an hour was lost that could have gone to completing the grant. He definitely did not appreciate her requesting a favor of him that put him at an inconvenience. Richard felt that Dr. Duncan showing up more than an hour late was a total disregard for his feelings. Dr. Duncan went up to her office with no apologies, just a cheerful "hello," as if she were right on time. Stephen strolled in at about 2:40 P.M. To Richard, it seemed that yet again, he was the only one who had some sense of responsibility to carry out a task.

Richard knew that this was no short task, but he only expected to come in for a few hours, help in whatever way he could, and then go home. Dr. Duncan did not inform him that preparing a grant was a much more tedious and time-consuming process than he expected. In addition to the typing of the 100 plus page grant, the group of four worked on graphs, and organized letters of support to accompany the grant. As the hours passed, and he worked away in a "zombie-like" mind state, Richard's anger subsided. He sat down to take a break, and looked over at one of the tables stacked with papers that was the product of a team effort slowly coming together. He stared in amazement at how much they had achieved in the time that they had been working there that day.

The Conclusion

At 8:30 P.M., Dorothy left to tend to a prior engagement. Stephen and Richard remained behind. Stephen continued working on the graphs, while Richard typed the remaining 50 or so pages of the written part of the grant.

Stephen finally stopped at 11:30 P.M. Richard stayed behind to organize the completed material and attempted to begin the remaining parts of the grant. Finally, after his wrists were cramped from the typing, his eyes were bloodshot red from staring at the computer monitor all day, and his legs were tired from running up and down the steps between Dr. Duncan's office and the office where he was working, Richard realized that he had to stop working for the day, to conserve enough energy to drive home. He threw in the towel at 5:00 A.M. Sunday morning. He was just too tired to go on. Dr. Duncan came downstairs to find some additional documents. She thanked him for coming in and they continued to talk in the office while Richard waited for security to unlock the doors.

As he left the building to return to the cold darkness that awaited him outside, he looked back on the day. He was surprised to realize how accomplished he felt. The feeling of accomplishing such a long and important task almost invigorated him to do it all over again. He was happy that his assistance was greatly needed, and that he was able to work with a team of people who, for that day, helped him step by step for as long as they could. He was happy to see the group, for once, giving their all to get the job done. He was happy that, for once, he was not the last person to leave, because someone else (Dr. Duncan) stayed behind to "carry the torch." He was happy that she even acknowledged his contribution with a simple thank-you, and a look as if to say, "I know that you work hard, and I really appreciate it." As he pulled out of the parking lot, he smiled, looked back at the building, and thought to himself, "Boy, and tomorrow is Monday."

Saving Private Ryan Video Case: Classic Leadership Models

by James C. Spee, University of Redlands

Case Overview

Saving Private Ryan tells the story of the D-Day invasion through the eyes of a schoolteacher turned warrior, Captain Miller. Its central story takes us on a journey that starts in a landing craft on Omaha Beach and ends with a pitched battle in a battered French village. Along the way, we meet paratroopers, glider pilots, prisoners of war, and a small platoon of soldiers sent to rescue the last surviving brother in a family of four. The other three brothers have died in the past week fighting in Europe and Asia. In its simplest interpretation, the mission to save Ryan is just a plot device to get us on the beach and then behind the lines to dramatize the way different groups of soldiers experienced the war. At a much deeper level, it asks us what risks we are willing to take to protect the things we hold dear.

Specific Teaching Objectives

You will learn to apply classic leadership models to your lives as managers using leadership examples from the film *Saving Private Ryan* (Spielberg, 1998). The following questions come from six classical leadership models:

- Trait theory (Stodgill, 1974)
- A behavioral model (Kerr, Schreisheim, Murphy, and Stodgill, 1974)
- Contingency theory (Fiedler, 1978)
- Normative theory (Vroom and Yetton, 1973)
- Path-goal theory (March and House, 1974)
- Transformational leadership theory (Burns, 1978)

Each theory can be taught using a different part of the film. Other leadership theories can be substituted at the instructor's discretion, but these six will be examined in this case.

Discussion Questions and Answers

1. First view the entire movie. Are the traits Captain Miller (Tom Hanks) displays as a leader in the film *Saving Private Ryan* consistent with those identified by trait models of leadership (Stodgill, 1974)?
    a. Does Miller show
        - achievement drive?
        - adaptability?
        - alertness?
        - ascendance?
        - attractiveness?
        - energy?
        - responsibility?
        - self-confidence?
        - sociability?
    b. What applications can you make to your life as a manager?

2. Review the Omaha Beach battle. Does Captain Miller exhibit the behaviors of a successful leader suggested by the behavioral model of leadership (Kerr, Schreisheim, Murphy, and Stodgill, 1974)?
    a. Does Miller exhibit behaviors related to relationship orientation?
        - Does he listen to group members?
        - Is he easy to understand?
        - Is he friendly and approachable?

- Does he treat group members as equals?
- Is he willing to make changes (Forsyth, 1983, p. 215)?

  b. Does Miller exhibit behaviors related to task orientation?
- Does he assign tasks to members?
- Does he make his attitudes clear to the group?
- Is he critical of poor work?
- Does he see to it that the group is working to capacity?
- Does he coordinate activity (Forsyth, 1983, p. 215)?

  c. What applications can you make to your life as a manager?

3. Review the second battle scene in which Miller's platoon meets up with a group of paratroopers in Neuville. Does Captain Miller change his leadership style in different situations consistent with the recommendations of the contingency model of leadership? How does Captain Miller rate on these three factors:

  a. Are leader/member relations strong or weak?

  b. Is task structure well defined or ambiguous?

  c. Does Miller have strong or weak leader position power?

Fiedler uses a measurement called the least preferred coworker (LPC) scale to determine whether a leader is primarily relationship motivated or task motivated.

  d. Does Captain Miller show more concern for task or for relationships with his followers?

  e. What applications can you make to your life as a manager?

4. Review the third battle scene in which the platoon attacks the machine gun nest next to a radar installation. Is Captain Miller's behavior consistent with the decision-making approach recommended by the Vroom-Yetton normative model of leadership? Is there a quality requirement such that one solution is likely to be more rational than another?

  a. Does Miller have sufficient information to make a high-quality decision?

  b. Is the problem structured?

  c. Is acceptance of the decision by subordinates critical to effective implementation?

  d. If Miller were to make the decision by himself, is it reasonably certain that it would be accepted by his subordinates?

  e. Do subordinates share the organizational goals to be attained in solving this problem?

  f. What applications can you make to your life as a manager?

5. Review the final battle scene, defending a bridge from German attack. Does Captain Miller provide the level of leader involvement that will result in the highest level of performance of his subordinates, according to path-goal theory (House and Mitchell, 1974)?

  a. What are Miller's subordinates' expectations?
- Do they expect autonomy?
- What is their level of previous experience?
- What is their level of ability?

  b. What are the key task characteristics?
- Is the task structured?
- Is the task difficult?

  c. Organizational structures may help or hinder leadership effectiveness.
- Do work group norms help or hinder Miller as leader?
- Do organizational rewards help or hinder Miller as leader?
- Do organizational controls help or hinder Miller as leader?

  d. What applications can you make to your life as a manager?

6. Review the opening and closing scenes of the old soldier at the Normandy cemetery. Burns (1978) defined transformational leadership and contrasted it with transactional leadership.
    a. Is Captain Miller a transformational leader?
        *   Does he motivate followers by appealing to higher ideals and moral values?
        *   Does Miller define and articulate a vision for their organization?
        *   Do Miller's followers accept his credibility as the leader?
    b. Does he also exhibit the characteristics of a transactional leader?
        *   Is Miller's leadership based on bureaucratic authority and legitimacy within the organization?
        *   Does Miller emphasize work standards, assignments, and task-oriented goals?
        *   Does Miller focus on task completion and employee compliance?
        *   Does Miller rely heavily on organizational rewards and punishments to influence employee performance?
    c. What applications can you make to your life as a manager?

References

Burns, J. M. (1978). *Leadership*. New York: Harper & Row.

Fiedler, F. E. (1978). The contingency model and the dynamics of the leadership process. In Berkowitz (Ed.) *Advances in experimental social psychology*. (Vol. 12) New York: Academic Press.

Forsyth, D. R. (1983). *An introduction to group dynamics*. Belmont, CA: Wadsworth.

House, R. J. and Mitchell, T. R. (1974). Path-goal theroy of leadership. *Journal of Contemporary Business*. 3:81–97.

Kerr, S., Schreisheim, C.A., Murphy, C. J., and Stodgill, R. M. "Toward a Contingency Theory of Leadership Based upon the Consideration and Initiating Structure Literature," *Organizational Behavior and Human Performance*. (August 1974) pp. 62-82.

Stodgill, R. M. (1974). *Handbook of Leadership*. New York: Free Press.

Vroom, V. H. and Yetton, P. W. (1973). *Leadership and decision making*. Pittsburgh: University of Pittsburgh Press.

The Safety Memo

by Gordon Baldwin

Gordon Baldwin, cable technician for the Cable Company, could feel the sweat begin to bead up on his forehead. His heart was beating rapidly as he sat uncomfortably in the lavish office chair. He could feel the tips of his ears burning. He opened his mouth to respond to a question but was quickly overwhelmed with the shouting erupting from Gil, the executive vice president of engineering. Gordon shifted uncomfortably in the chair. "Why doesn't he just fire me and get this over with?" Gordon thought. "How did this happen?" he wondered. "All this, just because I wrote a little safety memo."

Gordon's Background

After working 10 years for Pacific Bell, Gordon decided to resign from Ma Bell to pursue a career as a jeweler. As it turned out, this may not have been one of his better choices. Following several years of creating and repairing jewelry, he concluded that although precious metals and gemstones were fun to play with, one should not rely on them to support a family. Sensing that a career move was required, he considered his options. A return to telephone work seemed like the best idea, and Gordon sought to rejoin the phone company. Sadly, Pacific Bell was not hiring. So he contacted a local cable television firm and applied for a position. He was subsequently hired as a cable TV field technician.

The new employer was a very fast-paced, entrepreneurial, nonunion organization. Although this was in sharp contrast to the highly structured environment and strongly unionized workforce at the phone company, Gordon did not give it much thought at the time. This cable company was the twelfth largest in the nation and a subsidiary of a well-known *Fortune* 500 company. Gordon's new employer spanned the country. There were 2,700 employees, working in 30 offices, spread across 13 states, from Rhode Island to California. The company was dedicated to being the premiere broadband telecommunications provider of its time. Offering extraordinary customer service and building excellent internal employee relations were important business and cultural missions. Company representatives, during Gordon's new-hire orientation, frequently spoke about these.

Once on board, Gordon was given a truck, tools, and about two weeks of "ride along experience" with a seasoned employee to help break him in to the cable television business. Interestingly, the company did not give any formal training on how to perform important work operations safely. The lack of safety skills training on this job was in sharp contrast to the extensively detailed safety training he had received from the phone company. Although Gordon noticed the differences between each company's commitment to employee training, he did not think as much about this at the time as perhaps he should have. Fortunately, his duties as a cable television technician were quite similar to the telephone work he had performed for Pacific Bell. Because of this, he was able to utilize his former training to do the new job safely. However, just a few months into the new position, Gordon began to notice other employees taking life-threatening risks while using extension ladders, climbing telephone poles, constructing overhead lines, and doing other activities. He commented on these observations to his boss, Ron, and offered recommendations to help fix these problems. Gordon observed that the unsafe work practices that he pointed out to Ron continued to be used in the field, even though there seemed to be great interest in correcting these problems. Gordon mentally contrasted this with his former employer's immediate response to safety issues, but assumed the new company would begin to respond more quickly soon.

Contributing Events

Unknown to Gordon, events unfolding at the corporate office were working to heighten senior management's awareness of the need for a loss control program. First of all, Lawrence Walsh, CEO of the cable company, had become aware of a gap in his web of organizational control. He learned that for lack of a safety program at the operational level, his company was losing millions of dollars annually due to the costs of on-the-job injuries. Walsh was besieged by phone calls from the parent company's director of risk management. The director advised Walsh that some of his cable operations were operating at an OSHA rate of 23; this meant that annually, 23 percent of the workforce was sustaining a relatively serious and expensive injury on the job. This was obviously a situation of some concern. The CEO, who heretofore had focused on building market share and maximizing profits, was now pressured to find ways to stop escalating numbers of accidents and to rein in their costs. The parent company was also concerned about minimizing exposures to bad publicity and possible OSHA fines for unsafe workplace conditions and practices.

How Gil, the executive vice president of engineering, became involved in this situation is still unclear. It might have been because of the strong operational connection between Gil's engineering activities and the work done by field employees. It might also have been because of a request from his boss, Lawrence Walsh. As Walsh struggled to find a strategy he could implement to decrease safety losses, he may have looked to Gil for help. Walsh may have asked Gil to look into ways of dealing with the parent corporation's concerns. Walsh did not know of any special risk management skills that Gil had, but Walsh knew that Gil usually succeeded in accomplishing any missions he was given.

Also reporting to Walsh was Joan, a 33-year-old vice president of the southern California region. She was an involved manager, who wanted only safe and healthful work practices and conditions in her region. As a result of her own observations of safety problems, concerns raised by her staff, and encouragement from Walsh in the corporate office, she elected to become the sponsor of the southern California regional safety committee. She anticipated that the committee would help generate ideas and recommend practices to control runaway workers' compensation costs within the region.

Joan enlisted one of her management staff, Terry, to head her regional safety committee. Terry sought out volunteers from the region and began to form the committee. From time to time, Terry and Gordon would have the opportunity to talk about safety on the job. Terry passed along some of their discussions to Joan and she suggested that Terry enlist Gordon to serve on the safety committee. Terry discussed the safety committee idea with Ron, Gordon's boss, and it was decided to add Gordon to the committee, if he agreed.

A short time later, Gordon was asked to become system safety coordinator. This function was a collateral-duty assignment in which Gordon held two job responsibilities. Gordon was to spend about 60 percent of the week acting as a CATV service technician, and the balance of the week was to be spent on loss control activities. At Ron's request, Gordon prepared observations of job hazards, and made recommendations on a broad spectrum of safety concerns. These recommendations touched on delivering training, selecting equipment, issuing certifications, maintaining record keeping, preparing reports, ensuring employee involvement, and more. Gordon was told that he would be held accountable on his performance review for positively impacting the safety of other employees. Gordon's recommendations received good reviews and support from various managers in the organization, including leaders in the corporate office and at the regional headquarters.

Likewise, Ron was very supportive. However, Bob (Ron's manager) was unwilling to allow Ron to implement many of the recommended changes to improve safety. Bob voiced agreement in principle but allowed little corrective action to take place. In the meantime, Gordon was encouraged to conduct more research, review more company work practices, define more problems, and recommend more solutions. For some months, Gordon continued to do as he was asked. He observed that the only new safety processes that were implemented were the ones that did not involve spending money, or taking employees' time away from revenue-producing activities. He also noticed that it was difficult to gain an audience to discuss safety with some managers and supervisors. Gordon felt that this was due, in large part, to the lack of stature and authority carried by the safety coordinator's position, since he was only a technician.

As the weeks went by, Gordon found that movement toward implementation of safety training and adoption of safe practices and procedures was basically stalled by budgetary concerns and by slow acceptance of the need for these seemingly burdensome new practices. In counterpoint to this situation, Gordon felt strongly that his information was vital and timely. He had discovered that many of the managers with whom he worked were fundamentally unfamiliar with existing best practices and procedures for working safely in their own industry. Additionally, he saw that they were unaware of a substantial body of regulatory compliance requirements. Nonetheless, not much that was substantive was getting accomplished. Gordon was becoming frustrated as time passed.

What Happened

Around 10 A.M. one day in late September, the safety coordinator, Gordon, received a call from the administrative assistant to the general manager. She passed on a message from Bob, the general manager. Bob wanted Gordon to drop by the office. Not long thereafter, when Gordon was seated in Bob's office, the general manager produced a memo that Gordon had written about two weeks before. There was a handwritten note on the cover page, written by Gil, the executive vice president of engineering. The note directed Bob to have Gordon report to Gil's office in Orange County the following Monday morning.

Gordon asked Bob what was going on. He only made a general statement about how important it was to be careful about what one wrote in memos. He went on to say that someone had forwarded a memo (see appendix A) that Gordon had written, and Gil was concerned about some misleading statements. Now Gil wanted to talk to the guy who wrote it. Gordon was somewhat worried about this. He felt confident that he had not said anything that wasn't true. He was also sure that he presented his information honestly and reasonably. Deep down, he was afraid of being misunderstood and of losing his new job. He also prided himself in being able to communicate clearly and in being able to get along with most people. Therefore, he was very surprised at running into someone who seemed to have such a strong reaction against something that he had written.

Gordon had never met Gil, although he knew the executive by reputation. In the year since Gordon had been with the company, he had heard several "Gil Stories." They all described a huge, white-haired man, well over six feet tall, and weighing nearly 300 pounds, who was hard nosed and quick-tempered. Gil was rumored to be brutal in conducting company business. He was also reported to be without a shred of compassion. Gil could pin a man to the wall with his eyes and hold him there while he tore off flesh with his words. No one who knew Gil would ever think of getting on his bad side. If there was a choice between sitting across the desk from him when he was angry or sticking your hand in a blender, the choice was always the blender.

There were true stories that formed the basis for these rumors. For example, the preceding year, the company had purchased another firm in Arizona. On executive row at the California corporate office, the feeling was that there were probably too many employees working at the new Arizona location. Gil volunteered to "look into the situation." He did this by going to Arizona, putting a desk up in the middle of the main hallway, and stopping everyone who approached to ask them one question. The question was, "What do you do here?" If he didn't like the answer, he routed that person into a nearby room, where a human resources clerk was waiting with severance papers and a final paycheck. Gil reportedly eliminated 40 percent of the employees at the new office in less than three days.

Gordon had heard these stories from Gil's associates over the preceding months. The stories had been funny then. They were not funny now. The safety coordinator did not feel at all comforted by anything he had been told about the executive vice president. Gordon tried to do some research with those who had seemingly survived a confrontation with Gil. He asked an engineer on Gil's staff if there was anything he should say or do, or avoid saying or doing in the meeting with Gil. Gordon also asked if there were any "signs" by which he would know how much trouble he was really in. However, there were no clues to be read where Gil was concerned. One just went in, closed the door, and waited for the explosion.

In this case, the bomb burst slowly. Gil had a large and quiet office with lots of certifications and credentials in frames on the walls. He invited Gordon in and offered him a chair. Then, with the victim seated, Gil stood up. He started off speaking calmly, but soon, his voice became loud and irritated. As he got louder, his visitor became worried. Gordon's voice became frightened and small to his own ears. About this time, he noticed that Gil was really much closer to seven, or maybe even eight, feet tall. He was also much larger than described, at least 400 pounds. His eyes were very bright and piercing.

Gil shook the memo and asked, "Did you write this?"

Gordon answered, "Yes."

"Why did you write this?" Gil wanted to know.

"It was the result of research and a number of prior reports requesting help to correct some critical safety deficiencies," Gordon answered.

Gil demanded, "Don't you know that what you said is not true?"

"I'm unaware of anything in the memo being untrue," Gordon replied.

"If you were unaware, why did you go on to write something that was inaccurate?" asked Gil.

Gordon was getting confused. He knew the information was valid, yet the executive vice president seemed to be taking him in circles around the facts.

Gil continued, "I personally know of extensive company investments in accident prevention and I know we have top-level commitments to the safety of company employees. In fact, I've sponsored these myself. I know a great deal about safety on the job. I have no doubts that I know more about workplace safety and accident prevention in this industry than you do. After all, I've been committed to safety since the days when I drove an ambulance in the war, and I've seen, firsthand, how terrible the injuries can be when things go wrong. Therefore, not only am I fully committed to safety, but just who are *you* anyway, to come into this company, where I've worked for over 20 years, and write memos that accuse me of not taking safety seriously?"

Gil's voice was growing louder and louder. He was pacing behind his desk, then pausing to lean both arms on the desk and scowl down at Gordon. Gil was breathing harder and his face was flushed. Gordon was breathing hard too, from fear. His voice was shaking when he tried to talk. Fortunately, Gil was not listening to anything Gordon tried to say, so it is doubtful that he ever heard Gordon's quavering words. At least there wasn't any need to be embarrassed about that.

Gil growled and roared around his office for two hours. He repeated many times that he was personally insulted that Gordon would write a memo accusing him and the company of not being committed to safety, and not doing all that needed to be done to protect employees. As the meeting went on, Gordon had no doubts about any of Gil's feelings toward the memo, or toward Gordon himself. He was also very clear about Gil's position on the topic of personal insults—Gil did not like them at all. Additionally, Gil was making it painfully obvious that any future safety memos of that type would not be as well received as this one was!

At the same time as these realizations were dawning on Gordon, he mentally noted that he had given up trying to utter any complete sentence about 15 minutes into the meeting. He felt it might have made Gil angrier. Besides, Gil wasn't listening anyway. So, Gordon used his trembling voice as little as possible, mostly to grunt an affirmative or mumble, "Uuhh hunh."

At the end of about two hours, Gil glanced at his watch, lowered his voice, and sat down behind the desk. He calmly continued to speak, summarizing his concerns about putting things in writing that were not true and that might generate liability for the company. He concluded by asking if Gordon had any questions. The executive vice president then rose, extended his hand, and said that he hoped this meeting had been beneficial.

Gordon left the office a mere shell of a person. He could not ever remember feeling so devastated. He was in some kind of shock, in part because he did not realize that someone else could get inside of him and wreak such mental and emotional havoc. He felt really badly, very low, and totally worthless. He knew he was going to be fired, and hated Gil for torturing him for so long, only to have him fired later. But he also felt so miserable that the thought of getting fired made him feel better. For the rest of the week, he moped around work and home, still trying to analyze what had happened. The whole thing with Gil's anger and accusations seemed very wrong and completely unfair. The memo had not been full of untruths. Gil had never listened or really given him a chance to explain at all.

THE CABLE COMPANY

Date: September 8
Subject: Safety
From: Gordon Baldwin
To: Terry Jehlen

There is a need to have the company show as much genuine interest in its own safety program as it expects its employees to show.

The company should make an effort at the outset to appear serious about its program. A letter to all personnel from the president or chairman of the board would be an excellent beginning. Some additional needs would be:

- Regularly scheduled meetings.
- Meetings held in a comfortable but structured atmosphere, such as a conference room.
- Field training provided at a facility designed for the purpose.
- Courses required in such areas as defensive driving, pole climbing, first aid, CRR, GO 95, and more.
- Short tailgate-type meetings are necessary, but at the inception of a safety ''discipline,'' some attention to the impact of ''form'' is due.

In keeping with this thought, The Cable Company should have a program that is rich in resources. After all, the amount of training that has been overlooked is really staggering. The need for an accelerated ''catch-up" is obvious. This catch-up will be facilitated by an orderly acquisition and dissemination of information.

There must be an in-house organized information pool from which each system can access training material. When the immediate, basic safety training needs of the southern California operation have been addressed, this pool should also be able to assist the individual system with most of the special safety training needs it might have.

There is no one employed by the company who is legally exempt from safety training of some type. In addition to the training of field workers, The Cable Company should look at management training, supervisory training, office personnel training, and the related inspection activities such as regular building inspections, vehicle inspections, and equipment inspections as required by law.

There is a vast amount of information available to The Cable Company on safety. A major difficulty in assembling it is that only a portion of what is needed is available from any one source. Once finding a source, the time-consuming ritual of research begins.

    The demands of the safety organization within the company
will not grow less with time. Once established, the program must
be kept currently abreast of federal, state, and local laws. The
Cable Company must also remain up-to-date on changes in
technology as they affect the health and safety of the employees.
Formulating this information pool, maintaining it, and
disseminating it are very good reasons for establishing a full-
time safety coordinator.

    Having a safety program ''on paper only'' neither benefits
nor fools anyone. A management commitment is necessary to assume
the responsibility, take the time, and spend the money to provide
safety facilities, training equipment, and personnel. An
unwillingness to accede to the needs of a safety program in any
of these areas effectively kills the program.

cc: R. Kelso

Joan, Your thoughts? TSJ

Lawrence, I agree with Gordon but we must start somewhere and it begins with us.
JO
Cc: Mgmt Team

The Volunteer

by Louise A. Palermo

Linda Davidson really enjoyed her job as the coordinator of volunteers at the small but very well-visited museum. The museum was a facility of a rather large city but was located at its furthest boundaries. For the staff at the museum, this meant that contact with "city powers" was minimal and they felt enabled to do as they pleased, often circumventing the bureaucracy that was inherent in city governments. At first, this seemed like a positive circumstance to Linda as the very word *bureaucracy* had such a bad connotation. However, she soon realized that bureaucracy also had its benefits.

The museum was nestled on the shore of a lake that attracted many families for recreational purposes. Because there was no admission charge, the families would usually find themselves participating in many of the museum's educational activities designed for these groups. It also was a prime destination for schools whereby yearly over 85,000 school children were guided in special, interactive tours led by volunteers. In all, over 250,000 people utilized this small jewel each year.

Museum Staff

The director of this facility was Dr. Monroe, a small, inconspicuous woman who held a Ph.D. in biology. Although she was skilled in numbers, grant writing, and land mammals, she seemed very out of place at the helm of such a well-visited organization. In the second tier of command was Mr. Tanaka, also of diminutive stature and with a degree in biology. He proved to be lacking in management skill and it appeared to Linda that he achieved his level of success due to attrition as opposed to any real talent. Also on that level was Mrs. Phillips, an older woman savvy in city politics as she had been transferred from "downtown" and was still connected— when she felt the need.

Another very important level of this organization was a separate, powerful group called the "FRIENDS" of the museum. This organization contained the group of volunteers dedicated to the programs offered by the museum and raised over $350,000 each year in support. From that came Linda's salary. Mrs. Grant was the president of the volunteers, a supervisor to the volunteer coordinator, and it seemed to Linda, one more boss than the position needed!

City Mandate

As a 41-year-old white woman, Linda felt very lucky to have this position. She had not yet earned a bachelor's degree and had been out of the workforce for over 15 years in order to raise her two children. However, during this time away from the workforce, Linda spent several days each week volunteering and developing programs at schools and public interpretive centers. She felt passionate about helping her children become properly educated, and she felt the same about helping other children learn in a fun, safe, interactive way. That and the experience she gained in developing and teaching these programs were what gave Linda the idea that she would be very successful in the volunteer coordinator position. The museum seemed to offer a fun, safe, pleasant environment that encouraged learning and gave her the feeling that she belonged there.

After landing the job, Linda dove into it with exuberance. In reviewing old files, she discovered a pile of memos directed to Mr. Tanaka and the previous volunteer coordinator mandating formal registration and fingerprinting of all volunteers. As a mother, this made sense to Linda as it assured a level of integrity in the volunteer force thereby protecting the many thousands of children who visited the facility. Naively, wanting to do her best, Linda contacted the city. She was surprised when the voice on the city-end of the phone sounded relieved to hear someone willing to comply with the often repeated mandate, and immediately Linda was scheduled for training on the procedure. In excitement, Linda went to Mr. Tanaka with the news.

Mr. Tanaka was a man of many words, and it seemed to Linda he used every one of them to tell her in a convoluted way that she had done the wrong thing and this museum was not about to comply with such a time-consuming rule. He advised her to ignore the memo, as he had, that no one had ever followed that silly procedure, and if she left it alone, the city would soon forget about it.

Linda was confused, but she said nothing to Mr. Tanaka. She couldn't understand how he could see the fingerprinting as time consuming. She wondered what she should do since she had already registered to take the training. It just didn't make sense to her. She tried to reason it out by evaluating Mr. Tanaka's management style and personality. She knew he could be inconsistent in his decisions. Although he was in charge of over 20 people, he had no formal management training and tended to be very inconsistent in his policies. Many times Linda observed him making spur of the moment decisions only to forget what he had dictated and send that employee on an entirely different path. Many staffers were frustrated by his poor leadership but stayed because jobs in the museum field were scarce and the only competitor was being built by the neighboring city and not yet finished.

She also had observed that as an unmarried man, he felt no compunction in carrying on a personal relationship of a sexual nature with a much older female employee who was in his direct supervision. He loved to monopolize people's time with long, lopsided philosophical dissertations timed, usually, with their departure for home at the end of the day. Many employees were very late in going home as a result.

Linda felt that she was in a difficult position, but since she wasn't too impressed with Mr. Tanaka's management style or values and the reason he gave seemed irrational, Linda decided to quietly take the training and soon after, she began registering volunteers. Linda noticed that Mr. Tanaka did not say anything to her when she began fingerprinting the volunteers, but he did act reserved around her.

Felon Volunteer

About six months into her job, Linda was alone in the office she shared with Mr. Tanaka. A part-time volunteer coordinator who handled a seasonal program came into her office. Erica was responsible for recruiting and training the seasonal volunteers and explained that she had discovered that one volunteer who had been in the program for several years was problematic. This man wanted to return this year. Erica was very nervous as she told Linda this volunteer's history as a convicted child molester. He had spent seven years in jail. Unfortunately, he had numerous opportunities to be alone with children in this program and Erica was afraid.

Erica also explained that Mr. Tanaka had approached her and said that no matter what Linda had planned, there would be no fingerprinting for this group. He confided in Erica that he wanted to give a friend with legal problems a chance to be in the program. He told Erica he would be fully responsible and beyond that it was none of her business. Erica felt guilty for not speaking out sooner, but Mr. Tanaka was her boss and she really needed her job.

Linda was in shock. She couldn't believe the jeopardy in which the museum had been put. She knew she must speak to Mr. Tanaka.

Because she didn't want to incur his wrath, Linda tried to be casual in her approach. She knew he could be retaliatory. She had watched in disbelief as he withheld hours from an employee who had fallen out of favor with him. Since he was not fired, that employee could not collect unemployment. Neither could he live on the limited income.

Linda picked up the latest memo and asked Mr. Tanaka if she could review it with him. She explained the city was pretty firm about fingerprinting all volunteers. He took the memo from

Linda, placed it in his drawer, and told Linda not to worry about anything, as it was his responsibility.

Again, Linda decided that it was her responsibility to comply with the city mandate, so she went to a meeting of the seasonal volunteers intent on fingerprinting each one. She reasoned that when the prints came back as unacceptable, Mr. Tanaka would have to see reason. That night the felon lied to Linda and said he already had volunteer prints with the city. He refused to be printed again. With this Linda decided to go back to Mr. Tanaka and be more assertive. This felon was a danger to children and to the museum's reputation.

This attempt at reason with Mr. Tanaka found Linda at the receiving end of his shouting. He finished by clenching his teeth and saying, "Stay out of it! It is my responsibility!" Linda replied, "You don't understand. It is I who will be fired. You have 20 years with the city and they will never fire you. Then who will hire an inexperienced old lady like me? No one. And most importantly, I could never live with myself if a child were injured. You have to remove this felon." With this, Mr. Tanaka left the room. Linda sat down at her desk and documented the situation and as many conversations as she could clearly recall.

More Problems

Through a coworker later that week, Linda found out that Mr. Tanaka was complaining about the quality of Linda's work. He also began micromanaging Erica, many times bringing her to tears. The coworker who had shared the information, Dr. Monroe's secretary, even confided that she heard him tell Dr. Monroe that he didn't think Linda was doing such a good job. Linda found the felon at the next volunteer meeting fully instated by Mr. Tonaka.

In exasperation and with much trepidation, Linda went to Mrs. Phillips. She gave her all the details of the problem and asked for advice and intervention. She felt Mrs. Phillips might successfully convince Mr. Tanaka to do the "right" thing and the felon would be removed. She also told Mrs. Phillips she and Erica were afraid for their jobs so not to tell Dr. Monroe about the situation. Linda felt Mr. Tanaka easily manipulated Dr. Monroe and, again, Linda would be the one to incur consequences.

Later that day Mrs. Phillips did speak to Mr. Tanaka. The felon was released from the program. Mr. Tanaka stopped communication with Linda. From that point, he only spoke to Linda if people were present. Even when work depended upon communication, he would not speak to her. He also intensified the berating of Erica who was so overwhelmed that she quit.

Linda loved her job but felt that she was kept from performing it well. Mr. Tanaka was maligning her, and it seemed that some of the staff chose to believe the lies.

She thought things couldn't be worse the day Sally walked into her office. Sally was a small, youthful-looking woman in her early thirties who volunteered often. She had plenty of time as she was on medical disability, which kept her from steady work. Obviously shaken, Sally explained that until his removal from the program, she had been dating the felon. She pressed him for the reason of his removal and when he told her, she broke up with him. Now he had been stalking her and she was truly fearful. She retained a lawyer in a bid to get a restraining order and in doing so, the lawyer wanted an explanation of how the felon was able to get into such a program and serve for so many years.

Linda felt unprepared for this situation but thought carefully before she spoke. Once into court, the details would be public record. Any hungry reporter who collected the day's court proceedings would get wind of a molester and a museum. Linda knew this would be fatal to this small facility. Somehow she had to protect Sally and the children, keep her job, and repair her relationship with her boss.

Linda told Sally that she would do everything possible to support her, especially when she was on the museum premises. She also said that the reason that she did not inform Sally directly was because she had no cause until the felon refused fingerprinting. She did not tell Sally that she or any member of the staff had prior knowledge. Sally felt reassured and left the office for her day in court. Linda went to Mr. Tanaka and explained Sally's situation hoping to illustrate the problem caused by not screening volunteers.

Later that day, Linda overheard Mr. Tanaka commenting on Sally's disability to a room of employees. He stated that the problem was an emotional one, not physical. He went on to say that Sally had loose morals and was constantly making passes at him. Linda was livid.

When she found him alone, she explained to him once more the precarious position the museum was in and that this was now public record. She recommended that he tell Dr. Monroe everything before she, and the city managers, read about it in the paper. Mr. Tanaka said he did not see it that way; however, he would speak to Dr. Monroe. Linda watched as he went into the director's office and spoke to Dr. Monroe for over an hour. When he returned, he told Linda that Dr. Monroe was filled in on the entire incident.

The next day Mr. Tanaka was not at work. Linda found a photograph of the felon in an archive and decided to give it to Dr. Monroe for the security officers. Linda was very surprised when Dr. Monroe didn't have any idea what Linda was speaking about.

ORGANIZATIONAL CHART

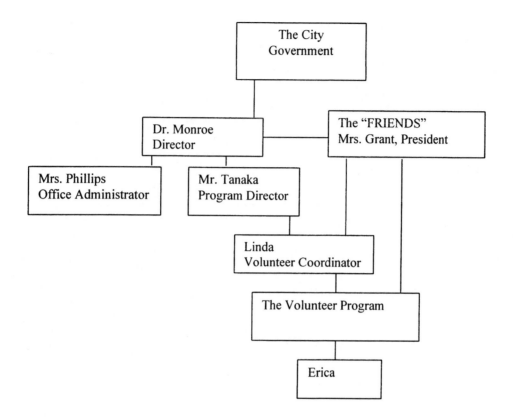

The Volunteer (B)

Linda was shocked to discover that Mr. Tanaka had not told Dr. Monroe anything about Sally, the felon, the restraining order, or any part of this incident. She gathered all records and shared them with Dr. Monroe. When Linda brought the documents in the room, Dr. Monroe told her that four years prior Mr. Tanaka approached her asking to bring the felon on board. The director made inquiries to the city lawyers who documented the question and answered, "NO!"

Armed with the present information, the director returned to the city lawyers who advised dismissing Mr. Tanaka. Because of his 20-year history with the city, Dr. Monroe interceded on his behalf and he was only restricted in his duties. This included removing Linda and her program from his supervisory role. Linda then reported only to Dr. Monroe and to Mrs. Grant. Linda was moved from Mr. Tanaka's office to a new one. The staff was extremely curious about what events could have possibly led to such an end when Mr. Tanaka had said Linda was so inept.

Since Mr. Tanaka no longer spoke to Linda, she found it increasingly difficult to do her job well. Despite the fact that she no longer shared his office or reported to him, he managed to reassign a large portion of Linda's job to a young female college student who did as she was told. Linda wondered if it was time to leave and what would become of the program with Mr. Tanaka continuing to make decisions.

Then There Was One

by Susan Pippert

It was November 1995, and Sarah had just returned from her honeymoon. Her honeymoon was so peaceful and relaxing, and she dreaded going back to work. During the past few months, there had been problems at work, and Sarah did not look forward to dealing with them. As a result of these problems, she wanted to find a new job because she no longer wanted to work in a department that was so closely monitored by upper management.

Sarah worked in a three-person human resources department, at a money management firm, which had 115 employees. For approximately three months, upper management regularly monitored the activities of Sarah, her boss—Mary, and her coworker—Ann.

Key Players

Sarah's boss, Mary, was in her early fifties, and held the position of human resources director. Mary had 20 years of experience in human resources, primarily in manufacturing. She had two years of experience with the company. One of those years was as a consultant, until the decision was made to hire her as a full-time employee. She did not have a college degree but was earning it through night school.

Mary always wore a suit and looked very professional. Her manner was rather quiet, even-tempered, and methodical. She never acted impulsively, and advised others to act like a cat—be very patient, and strike when your time comes. Though, when there was a problem, Sarah perceived Mary to deal with it more reactively than proactively.

Sarah's coworker, Ann, was in her early forties, and held the position of human resource manager. Ann had eight years of experience at the company, and was hired when there were only 30 employees. She started as an administrative assistant, then was promoted to office manager, and finally ended up in human resources. She had little formal human resources experience, but she knew the history of the company, and had handled many of the human resources functions before the department was formed. Ann had a bachelor's degree and was working on her master's degree in psychology.

Ann was very intelligent, though not perceived well by others in the company, primarily by some managers. She was referred to as "Norma Rae," which she considered a compliment, though it was not meant to be. She was very liberal and supported the employee, whom she perceived as the underdog. The company was very conservative and expected Ann to look after its interests.

Sarah, who had worked for the company for almost three years, was hired fresh out of college. She started three days after her graduation as an intern in human resources performing clerical functions and, after a few months, the decision was made to hire Sarah as a human resources assistant. She reported to Mary and also worked with Ann. They were instrumental in keeping Sarah on the fast track to training. During that time period, Sarah was primarily responsible for the daily functions of the department.

Tom, president and owner of the company, was in his mid-fifties and held the most powerful role in the company. He was very trusting of his top-level managers and perceived them as experts in their field, and never doubted their abilities, unless they made some obvious mistakes. If, and when, Tom got involved with a performance problem of his managers or other subordinates, at that point, termination would be initiated.

Background Information

One of the problems in the office was conflict. Mary often made mistakes, which put her in constant conflict with the director of compliance and with the controller, who were both well-respected individuals. Both of these individuals perceived Mary as incompetent. One of these "mistakes" occurred when the director of compliance and Mary met to discuss the severance details of a layoff. Mary drafted the severance agreement, with the most important details being wrong. Unfortunately, the agreement had already been presented to the employee and could not be changed. In retrospect, clear boundaries had not been established to outline the responsibilities of Mary and the director of compliance. Though they both reported to Tom, the president did not want to get involved and hoped they would work this out themselves. The conflicts between Mary and the controller were similar. The controller would tell Mary about a new procedure, and Mary would misunderstand, and end up making a major mistake. Lastly, Mary made mistakes on projects that Tom gave her. He would ask her to complete a project, and she would either take too long to complete the project, or the project would not meet Tom's specifications.

Another problem in the human resources department was confidentiality. Ann was viewed as a gossip because she sometimes failed to keep matters confidential. Often, when she found out confidential information, she secretly told the employees who would be affected. The department was eventually blamed for any confidential information that was leaked. In some cases, the department was blamed for information that Ann had never been told.

Because of these problems, Sarah grew weary of being associated with a department that had such a bad reputation. She worried that people viewed her as they did Mary and Ann. In addition, new projects had been halted, and Sarah began to feel stagnant in her job. She enjoyed and wanted new challenges, such as working on upward appraisals, and job classification evaluations, though in the last three months, both of these projects were stopped. She also felt that she did not have the autonomy she needed to grow. Often, she would meet with employees and listen to their problems. Sarah would consult Mary with her suggestions to get her feedback. Mary would then take Sarah's solution and deal with the employee herself. Sarah wanted the opportunity to learn by dealing with the employee from start to finish.

It was these factors that persuaded Sarah to find a new job. She also feared that, eventually, management would omit the problems in human resources by outsourcing the department or terminating positions. Sarah did not want to stick around to see what would happen. In spite of her decision and the problems, she liked both Mary and Ann very much as people. Sarah appreciated what they had taught her, which had helped her career.

The Critical Incident

Two weeks after Sarah returned from her honeymoon, Tom invited her to lunch. Because the company was small, and the department reported to him, this was not too unusual. She was a little suspicious of his invitation because his assistant was vague about the reason for their lunch. When Sarah got in the car, she could sense something was wrong, and she felt a huge pit in her stomach. She thought she was going to be fired, especially since she was a little preoccupied the previous month with her wedding. Sarah knew she had not been as productive as usual but had not been so preoccupied that she failed to complete important projects on time. The car ride to the restaurant felt like an eternity. She could not stand the waiting. She then realized that Tom would not take her to lunch to fire her, because Mary would fire her. Suddenly, she thought she knew what was coming.

When they arrived at the restaurant, she asked Tom why they were meeting. He told her he had some bad news. Sarah felt her heart pound for what seemed like an eternity. Then he told her that the company had decided to lay off Mary and Ann. Sarah's emotions overwhelmed her, while she remained speechless. In her concern for Ann and Mary, she almost forgot to ask how she would be affected. Sarah asked Tom where she would be working. He explained that the department would be outsourced and that she would be the on-site representative. She would be in charge, for the most part, and there would be a contact company to help her with any questions she had or projects that needed to be completed. She would report to the manager of reception and office services, and the head of operations.

Furthermore, Tom told Sarah that their department meeting scheduled for the next day would still take place, and that Ann and Mary would be terminated at that time. Sarah was a little bothered that he assumed she would attend the meeting and wait for him to ask her to leave before he fired them. She was in shock and somewhat angry because Ann and Mary would be under the impression that this was going to be a regular meeting and, wham, they would find out the horrible truth. Sarah was sad that two people, whom she considered to be more than coworkers, were going to lose their jobs. Because both of them had families, she felt they were very dependent on their salaries.

Then Sarah became a little excited about the change. She could now remain at a company she liked very much, in a respectable environment, with the opportunity to learn at an even faster pace. Soon that feeling subsided and turned to sheer terror. She feared her ability to handle the job alone. She questioned her experience in certain areas, such as employee relations, recruiting, and so on. At that moment, she really regretted that Tom chose to take her to lunch to deliver the bad news. Sarah could hardly eat. The emptiness and quiet atmosphere of the restaurant only magnified the silence between them. She would have preferred Tom to tell her the news in his office. Unfortunately, that was not the case, and they started to focus on life after the layoff.

After lunch, Sarah went back to work. She had to face Mary and Ann, and, though she was careful not to act too differently, it was difficult to act normal. She worried about being perceived by them as cold and callous, once they became aware that their jobs had been eliminated. She also worried about how they would feel if they found out that Sarah had been informed of their termination ahead of time. Sarah and Tom agreed that she would not report to work the next day. This way, Sarah did not have to be there when they were terminated. Her only regret would be the illness she would feign with Mary the next morning.

That night Sarah was really sad. She was going to miss interacting with Ann and Mary on a daily basis. Then she worried about reporting to a new supervisor and the kind of relationship they would have. Everything was soon going to change. She realized how ignorant she had been in the past, when others were in similar situations. On the other hand, her new supervisors were well respected within the company, and she hoped this would help when implementing new policies and procedures. In the past, it had been very difficult to get approval from Tom. However, if he supported the competency of his managers, he was more apt to implement one of their ideas.

The next morning, Sarah was so nervous, she did not know what to do. The meeting was scheduled to take place at 9:30 A.M. At 11:00 A.M., Sarah received a call from Mary and Ann. They were at Ann's house and wanted to let her know what happened. Sarah confessed that she had known the day before and offered them an apology. They were very nice and did not blame Sarah at all. Next they told Sarah what happened at the meeting.

Tom sat them down, and told them that there was going to be a layoff. Mary and Ann asked who would be laid off, and what could they do to help facilitate it. Tom explained that they would be laid off. At first, they thought he was joking. After a minute or so, when nothing was said, they realized that he was not joking. They both were in shock. Tom told them the reason for the layoff was because of the size of the company. Economically, he contended that it was more beneficial to keep one person, Sarah, and use an outside firm for anything else.

Mary was convinced that the director of compliance and the controller blackballed her and were able to convince Tom to eliminate the department. She was angry and felt betrayed. She was worried about her finances, since she was the breadwinner in her family. She was unemployed for a year before she got the human resources job, and she feared the difficulty of finding another one. Mary claimed she was not aware that people doubted her competence. She told Sarah that, typically, it is difficult to get management to approve any new policies. Furthermore, she said that most human resources people only last at a company for two to three years because, eventually, someone blames everything on the director, and she or he gets fired.

Ann, on the other hand, could not believe that after eight years she was getting laid off. Ann did not like the corporate world. In the past, she worked at nonprofit organizations and felt she fit in the best at those companies. Because of this feeling, she had already begun work on her master's degree in psychology and had begun to volunteer the required hours necessary to be a licensed therapist. She was extremely busy because she was working 40 hours a week, studying in the evenings, and working 20 to 30 hours a week doing psychology-related internships. She also had three children to mother. The severance she received gave her the opportunity to finish school and get her hours without having to worry about work. She said it was the perfect opportunity for her, and she was able to look at this experience as a good thing.

Life After the Layoff

Later that week, after the layoff, there were many meetings to discuss what changes would be made. Sarah delegated many of her responsibilities to free up her time for more important tasks. She was amazed at how everyone worked to develop her new job around the aspects she liked. One of the changes initiated was empowering the managers to make more HR decisions. In the past managers had to go through human resources for increases, new hires, and so on. This changed, allowing managers to get their manager's approval for these decisions. Sarah agreed with the changes because she could not do the quantity of work that was previously designed for three people. The workload was delegated to the accounting department and other managers. For example, hiring and salary negotiations now went to line managers. Sarah consider herself open to change and knew that there were better ways to run an HR department but, at times, found herself clinging to the old HR ways, and not "thinking outside the box." To completely disregard much of what she had learned was not as easy as she thought, but after time it started to get easier.

During the months after the layoff, Sarah moved her office and sorted through all of Ann and Mary's things. It wasn't long before she created a manager's handbook and revised the employee handbook. For the next few months, she worked 9- to-10-hour days. There was a lot of work to do, and she really enjoyed it. What Sarah discovered, during this process, was that she knew much more about human resources than she thought she did. She realized that she had the knowledge all along and just lacked self-confidence. Sarah gave a workshop for all managers, and presented the manager's handbook that she had created. She facilitated the meeting by explaining the new procedures and their rationale. It was at this meeting that Sarah realized the amount of information that she had retained about labor law and other areas related to human resources. She thought the managers were also surprised.

Many people came up to Sarah after the meeting and told her how impressed they were. Their accolades made Sarah feel good about her accomplishments and herself. From that meeting on, she maintained the confidence to do her job. When managers asked her opinion about a situation and acted on her advice, it was a joy. In the past when she gave her opinion, they would go to Mary to determine what they would actually do.

Two years later, the department remained with one person, Sarah. She continued to work hard and autonomously. She eventually adjusted to finding information on her own and working with an external mentor. The only challenge that remained was having a back-up person when she was out of the office. Over all, Sarah continued to hone her skills in human resources. This, coupled with her ability to survive in a sink or swim situation, proved to make her a better employee.

Unprofessional Conduct

by Andre Hamilton

Finding a Career

Andre Hamilton was feeling confident about his future. He had just spent eight years in the United States Air Force. While in the service, he learned how to conduct himself in a professional manner and, more importantly, he learned to respect others. To strengthen his chances of reaching his goal of becoming a manager, he completed a bachelor's degree in organizational management at the University of LaVerne. He always believed that graduating from college made a person more competent and understanding of the adversity and struggles of people. After graduating from school, his confidence soared to a point where he felt he was in a position of great demand by potential employers.

He was happy during conversations with some of his military friends as they talked about their decisions to return to school and to get their degrees. They listed what they thought were some of the best companies to work for, including PepsiCo, Coca-Cola, Hershey's, Toys 'R' Us, Home Depot, and The Office Supply Store (name disguised). During those days after graduating from school, Andre felt a solid sense of confidence.

The feeling reminded him of a song he liked, from a rap group called Bone Thugs–N–Harmony. The song was particularly uplifting to him, because it talked about how many young black men die and how society doesn't care. The uplifting feeling he got from this story was how he shared the same lifestyle of many of the men described in the song, yet he still managed to graduate from college.

Job Fair

In 1996, while looking through Sunday's *Press Enterprise* newspaper, he saw an ad for a job fair. He felt that he was in demand and that he would make a great employee for some potential company. Thinking of the companies that would be present at the job fair, he decided to attend.

The day of the job fair arrived. Upon arrival, he felt fear rush throughout his chest. There were so many people he would have to compete with for the jobs that were available. His interviews came down to two companies, G.M.A.C. and The Office Supply Store. Both interviews went extremely well.

G.M.A.C.

On Friday, September 27, 1996, Andre was interviewed by Mrs. Jane Apple from G.M.A.C., a mortgage company. At the interview, she explained to him the responsibilities of a loan officer, the position he had applied for. She also asked him questions about what he thought about the company. He told her he thought the company was great and appeared to be a good place to work. Mrs. Apple continued, informing him that although the position only paid commission, she felt he would have no problem earning a very lucrative salary. Mrs. Apple looked at Andre and said, "You have the job if you want it." He was thrilled and tried hard to contain his happiness. He told her he would accept her offer and thanked her for giving him an opportunity. When he left her office and got home, he immediately informed everyone he knew about his new job.

On Monday, September 30, 1996, when he arrived at work, he was greeted and introduced to the staff members and shown around the office. Mrs. Apple told him to relax and look around the office while she attended a quick meeting and got caught up on her messages.

As he walked around the office in his new place of employment, he began to feel that he had accomplished his goal of becoming a career person with a good job. Everyone was very friendly and seemed happy to be employed at that company. What he enjoyed the most about this organization was the team style of leadership displayed by Mrs. Apple.

The Office Supply Store

On Tuesday, October 1, 1996, he had his second interview with The Office Supply Store. He was interviewed by Mr. Smith, district manager, and Maria Smith, human resources director. They were very pleasant and energetic, and he got the impression that the work environment at The Office Supply Store was the same as he had experienced at G.M.A.C.

After the interview, he was told he had the position and would receive a letter in the mail telling him the pertinent information and the store where he would be working. He decided to accept the job offered from The Office Supply Store, because he wanted to move into management (the position he had gotten his degree in). In addition, he was concerned that, at G.M.A.C., he had to rely on commission as his only income, while at The Office Supply Store, he would have a steady salary. He also liked the close location to his home. He was very pleased because The Office Supply Store would train him to manage his own store. He thought of how nice it would be to eventually work his way up to district manager in this company.

On Wednesday, he returned to G.M.A.C. and asked Mrs. Apple if he could have a word with her in private. She agreed and they went into her office and sat down. He immediately got right to the issue and informed her that he had been made an offer by The Office Supply Store and that he felt it would be a better opportunity for him. She listened to what he had to say and sounded sincere when she informed him that she hated to see him go but understood why he had come to his decision. Ending the conversation, she told him that if it didn't work out at The Office Supply Store, he should call her and she would gladly give him another opportunity. Andre thanked her and told her that he really appreciated her sincerity and left. As he left, he had a sense of apprehension leaving such a warm environment to go to an unknown one.

Unprofessional Conduct

After receiving the letter telling him where to report to work, he arrived at his training store. Andre was to meet with the general manager who was also his new boss. When he walked into the store, he asked a cashier where he could find Mrs. Richards, the general manager. She directed him to the rear of the store to a small office. When he reached the general manager's office, he saw a middle aged female sitting at her desk. He introduced himself and informed her that he was Andre and that he was sent to this store by the district manager to begin his management training.

Andre froze as he noticed her face begin to flush. She just stared at him with a blank look of frustration and puzzlement. "Why are you here? You are supposed to be at the orientation meeting in Chino," she said sharply.

He informed her that according to the letter he received from the district manager he was to report to this store and was not told of any orientation meeting. He reached into his briefcase and retrieved the letter that was sent to him by the district manager and gave it to her for examination.

After she examined the letter, she began yelling, "They should not have sent you here," and continued saying that she couldn't figure out why some "ass-hole" had messed up the letter. She then asked him to have a seat in the break area next to her office, while she straightened out the situation over the phone.

After meeting the general manager and observing her behavior, he began to get angry at the nasty language she was using. He felt this showed a total lack of professionalism. He began to wonder where she received her training as a manager. He shivered at the thought of having to deal with this type of attitude on a daily basis.

Andre remembered how he felt about his first day at G.M.A.C., and how pleasant the manager and employees were. He didn't feel wanted at The Office Supply Store. He wondered if Mrs. Richards had someone else in mind to fill the position.

The more he thought about his reception, the angrier he became. He even thought about punching her in her face or engaging her with some profanity of his own, since that was obviously the type of behavior she was used to. It seemed to him that her behavior and action demonstrated a total lack of respect for him as an employee and human being. He thought of the song he liked from the rap group Bone Thugs–N–Harmony. In particular he remembered the part where they rapped about how society doesn't care about young black men. When he compared her behavior to the words of this song, he just viewed her as another member of society that had a chip on their shoulders about young black men. After he evaluated this incident using the song as inspiration, he began to feel better, knowing he could overcome this obstacle in a positive way as well.

In looking at possible options he had in this situation, he thought of as many as he could to give himself a fair opportunity in resolving the situation. His first option was definitely to punch her in the face, but he knew that would result in trouble with the police. He realized he couldn't give in to his feelings of anger, even though he felt that she was trying to degrade him.

Another option was just to walk out the door, but he took the attitude that he would overcome this and proceeded to convince himself that this was an isolated event. He felt this was the standard "grin and bear it" method of maintaining a job.

After he had calmed down, he viewed the situation from a more practical perspective. He told himself that he should probably just start looking for another job. He then thought of confronting her about her behavior and attitude, and appealing to her sense of decency. But he decided he should remain silent on this issue, because he had continuously heard people say throughout the years "don't rock the boat."

Finally, the last option he thought of was to go talk with the district manager about his experience, but he quickly dismissed that thought fearing, that as a new employee, the district manager's natural reaction would be to defend Mrs. Richards's behavior, and label him with an attitude problem. So, he did nothing.

Over the next few weeks, the general manager continued to display the same level of behavior, which became totally unbearable. Andre even tried, feeling very much at risk, to communicate with her as two mature adults. To his disappointment, he felt that she appeared uncaring and uncooperative.

What to Do?

At The Office Supply Store, there were no channels that would allow a person to change positions without penalty. He just couldn't go the district manager and request reassignment. He felt isolated without social support.

Andre was in misery because Mrs. Richards was so rude and abrasive. After a couple of weeks, he strongly reconsidered the possibility of discussing this matter with the district manager. But he was convinced, given the statement the manager had made several times that "she was the best trainer he had," that his concerns would be disregarded. In his past experience in the military and other places of employment, he observed that it had been pretty much standard practice to label complainers as troublemakers. Thus, he felt that talking with the district manager was not a viable option.

Andre was besieged with self-doubt. He reflected on questions such as the following: "Should I stick it out and hope to work for a decent boss eventually, or should I bail out now? Am I really cut out for this work? I wonder if I'm so touchy because I really don't want to be here anyway. Other people have put up with abuse from their boss, why can't I? If I leave here, will I just be unhappy somewhere else? Did I really think about what I wanted in a career, or did I leap too soon and take any job with a company that had a good reputation? Am I cut out for retail sales?"

Violence at the United States Postal Service:

The Killing of James Whooper by Bruce Clark (A)

by Diane R. Layden, University of Redlands

In the early morning hours of Sunday, July 9, 1995, postal worker Bruce William Clark shot and killed his supervisor, James Whooper III, at the U.S. Postal Service Processing and Distribution Center in City of Industry, California, just east of Los Angeles. Whooper was the thirty-fifth postal worker to die in a workplace violence incident between 1983 and 1995.[1] Both Clark and Whooper were long-term employees with excellent employment records, and the City of Industry facility was said to be a model facility for employees by postal and union officials alike.

The Killing of James Whooper

The City of Industry, California, Processing and Distribution Center is a 24-hour operation. In July 1995, 1,000 workers processed 5 million pieces of mail per day, and another 1,800 letter carriers worked out of the station.[2] According to Thomas Wilson, facility manager, postal officials recently praised his plant for having the fewest employee grievances, and employees gave it high marks as a good place to work. Indeed, Miguel Rodriguez, an area official of the American Postal Workers Union (APWU), said he thought this plant was the last place at which a shooting would occur. The facility was the site of a special program that allows employees more decision-making authority in an effort to increase morale. Over the entrance hung a banner that states, "This is a mail handler and management quality of working life postal facility—best postal service in the whole world just got better!"

On July 9, 1995, James Whooper, age 50, was working as a relief mail processing supervisor. He had been employed by the Postal Service for almost 33 years and earned an annual salary of $47,283. In late May 1995, Whooper transferred to the City of Industry facility from the Rosemead facility, where he supervised letter carriers. He wanted to work at night so that he would be able to provide assistance to his elderly mother during the day. Previously, he worked in Los Angeles until 1992, when his position was consolidated as a part of the reorganization and downsizing of the Postal Service. Whooper was a member of the Army Reserve and spent two weeks on reserve duty after his transfer to the City of Industry facility.

Bruce Clark, age 58, was a distribution clerk who sorted mail. He had been employed by the Postal Service for 22 years, with over 17 years at the City of Industry facility. He earned $35,604 annually. Clark had served in the Vietnam War. He held a master of science degree in mathematics, and had taught math in college for a few years earlier in his career.

Between 1:30 and 2:00 A.M., postal employee Robin Ross saw Clark walk to the supervisor's desk where Whooper was standing and deliver an unprovoked, clenched, double-fisted blow to the back of Whooper's neck. Ross rushed over and restrained Clark by holding one arm, while Whooper held Clark's other arm. Clark's face was red. Ross asked Clark several questions, and in response Clark stated that he was okay, that he did not have a gun, and that he was able to return to work. Clark appeared to be coherent, and Whooper instructed him to go back to work.

At about 2:00 A.M., Whooper called Edward Brassell, acting manager of the facility, who joined Whooper at his location. Between 2:15 and 2:25 A.M., Clark was seen walking from the area near the men's locker room toward the workroom floor. The locker room was located between the workroom floor and the employee parking lot. An electronic badge reader was located at the entrance from that parking lot to the building. According to the printout from the reader, Clark entered the building at 2:21 A.M. Deputies from the Los Angeles County Sheriff's Department (LASD) later found Clark's car in the parking lot.

At about 2:30 A.M., as Brassell and Whooper were talking, Brassell saw Clark approaching them. Clark had his right hand in a paper bag. Brassell called out to Clark and asked him what was in the bag. Clark did not say anything. Brassell again asked Clark what was in the bag. Again, Clark did not say anything. Clark pulled a gun out of the bag. Brassell began to run, and he looked back over his shoulder to see Clark proceed directly toward Whooper. Whooper backed up toward a letter-sorting machine and shouted, "No!" Whooper tried to leap backward over one of the consoles of the letter-sorting machine, but he landed on top of the console. Clark pointed the gun at Whooper's face and shot. Brassell saw the gun flash and smoke, and he turned away. Brassell heard a second shot and turned around to see postal employee Patrick Joseph McDonnell grab Clark. Whooper fell to the floor and died.

Many of the people in the building dived under desks or fled. McDonnell wrestled with Clark and got the gun. As his coworkers subdued him, Clark allegedly cried: "Did I get him?"[3] When the deputies arrived, Clark was asked if there was anyone else in the building with a gun; he replied, "I'm the one responsible for this. There is nobody else." Deputies searched the building but did not find anyone else who was involved in the murder.

Paramedics pronounced Whooper dead at 2:57 A.M. The coroner's investigator determined that one bullet entered Whooper just over the left corner of his mouth, appeared to proceed along his jaw, and exited through his left ear. A spent round of ammunition was recovered from the console that Whooper had been trying to leap over when Clark shot him. The second shot, for which there was no exit wound, had entered the left side of Whooper's chest. An autopsy concluded that the gunshot to Whooper's torso was fatal because it perforated his left lung, heart, aorta, spine, and spinal cord. A .38 caliber revolver bullet was removed from Whooper's vertebra.

The gun was a five-shot .38 Special Smith and Wesson revolver. Two rounds were spent and three unused rounds were left inside the gun. The deputies recovered the paper bag near Whooper's body, which had a fingerprint that was identified as belonging to Clark. At the LASD substation, Clark stated, "What I did, I did alone. Just so you know, I didn't intend to hurt anyone else. I just had the one person in mind." After giving the Postal Inspection Service (PIS) permission to search his home, he told postal inspectors they would find ammunition for the gun and papers that provided evidence of premeditation, apparently referring to his investigation of Whooper. They did not find the papers but found the ammunition and a hand-drawn street map of the neighborhood where Whooper lived.

Clark was charged with felony murder, murder of a postal employee, and use of a firearm during a crime of violence. In January 1996, after motions by his attorney to suppress evidence and statements were denied, Clark pleaded guilty to second-degree murder and use of a firearm. In May 1996, he received the maximum sentence of 22.5 years in prison, without possibility of parole. According to a newspaper account of the hearing, U.S. Attorney Patricia Donohue "said Clark gave no motive for the shooting and showed no remorse. [Clark] sat silently during the hearing. He kept his eyes focused on the courtroom wall and did not look at those testifying. He declined to address the judge. No relatives or friends of Clark were in the courtroom."[4]

Because Clark has not disclosed his motive for killing Whooper, one may only speculate as to his motive. Clark told his closest friend, William Windle, that he was "singled out" by his supervisor and asked Windle to check Whooper's license plate number. Also, Clark employed a private detective to investigate Whooper. He told the detective that he disliked his supervisor, he believed he had a criminal past, and he wanted him terminated. The plea agreement signed by Clark, which was written by U.S. Attorney Donohue, stated that Clark attacked Whooper because he "perceived that he was a threat to other postal employees." It was the theory of the prosecution that Clark killed Whooper because Whooper disturbed the balance of relations in Clark's social world. Another consideration is that Whooper's relatives alleged the crime was racially motivated, in that Clark is white and Whooper was an African American. Clark's attorney contended the facts of the case show that the killing had no racial motive.

Comments by Observers

At the time of the shooting, according to newspaper accounts, all observers were at a loss to explain Clark's behavior.[5] There was no evidence that Clark was under the influence of drugs or alcohol, and investigators found no indication of conflict between Clark and his boss or coworkers.

Both employees were said to have "blemish-free" records. Postal Service officials described Whooper as a soft-spoken, progressive, and nonconfrontational supervisor. However, Omar Gonzalez, an APWU official, said Whooper was a strict disciplinarian. He described him as mild-mannered and a nice person but a strict supervisor: "When he was in Los Angeles, there were problems with him. He was overly stern and heavy-handed." Gonzalez said the union at one point brought the issue of Whooper's management style before a labor-management meeting, but he could not recall specific grievances, and said that he may have changed once he got out of the major plants in Los Angeles. Union officials did not recall any problems after he transferred to the Rosemead and City of Industry facilities. Gladys Hoy, a postal worker in Los Angeles who was Whooper's former girlfriend and the mother of his son, also said that he was a strict manager: "He only did his job. He went strictly by the book. But James was not the type of person who would provoke anyone."

Thomas Wilson, City of Industry postal facility manager, described Clark as a very quiet, unassuming gentleman who reported to work on time and had no record of disciplinary problems. Although coworkers said they had little indication that Clark was disgruntled, he had complained to his friend William Windle that a supervisor at work had singled him out for discipline. Windle, who had been Clark's neighbor since 1991, said Clark was not a disgruntled postal worker, but he had "deteriorated emotionally" after 22 years on the job. With respect to Clark giving him Whooper's license plate number, Windle said, "He wanted me to try and find out something about the guy. The guy had singled him out and he didn't know why. But . . . he really loved his job."

Clark lived in Azusa. His neighbors said he was quiet and did not cause any problems. The attack was said to be "totally out of character." Windle, an apartment supervisor, said Clark often came to his home on Sundays and they talked about life: "Bruce just loved life. He lived alone and he didn't have many friends. Still, sometimes the guy aggravated me because he loved everybody. I'd tell him how many of my tenants would drive me crazy and he'd say 'Aw, they're good people.'" Clark was known as the "Cat Man" because he cared for so many stray cats. On the cul-de-sac where Clark lived, neighbor Pauline Skeldon said that when she first heard news reports of the incident, she thought Clark was the victim and was shocked to learn that he was the aggressor: "He'd feed all the stray cats in the neighborhood, and he was such a good worker. I just didn't realize he had that kind of a temper. He was so easygoing." Another neighbor, Lilly Lopez, agreed: "He was a little old, fragile and quiet for that. He is very quiet, very clean, very concerned. If people got hurt, he'd be there." One neighbor, Jon White, said that Clark's cats were his main family. His only contact with Clark was when his neighbor stopped by to see if one of his missing cats had strayed into White's camper: "It seemed like he wouldn't recognize you as a person. He would just come over to look for his cats."

Whooper lived on a different cul-de-sac in Rancho Cucamonga some 25 miles away. Neighbors said he liked to ski on winter weekends and was a favorite of the teenagers because he paid them well to water his lawn while he was away. He was described as a "nice guy" who had no enemies.

The Prosecution's Theory of the Case

Thomas Dugan, who led the investigation for the PIS, conducted more than 30 interviews at the City of Industry facility. Both Clark and Whooper were described as "likable, decent people." No one mentioned a racial motive for the shooting. Clark was portrayed as extremely shy and a "loner." He seemed to have no interests outside his cats and his job at the Postal Service. Clark earned excellent work ratings and achieved 100 percent accuracy on his last few tests. Coworkers said he was not the fastest worker, but he was steady; he "cleared his area." The work he did was "mechanical," that is, repetitive, but chatting with coworkers was permitted. Clark was considered a "sweet old character." He had a circle of six to ten acquaintances, none of whom associated with him outside the workplace. Several acquaintances were women, who were Asian Americans or Pacific Islanders. He carried heavy objects for them, although this was against the rules. He frequently gave gifts of cookies and candy to the women on his tour (shift) and tried to win stuffed animals for them from a machine on the premises.

Whooper was described as an outgoing person and a conscientious supervisor. He spent his eight-hour tour looking into every operation because he was new to his assignment and was trying to learn it in an effort to do a good job. He walked around the workfloor and made notes about employees and their duties. Some employees found him to be more "removed" as a boss than former supervisors had been (no further information was provided regarding Clark's former supervisors). No one interviewed said that Whooper was abusive or that he was "cracking down" on the weekend middle-of-the-night shift, but he was "around a lot" and some employees felt he was "looking over their shoulders."

As stated earlier, the plea agreement authored by the prosecuting attorney stated that Clark killed Whooper because "he perceived that he was a threat to other postal employees." The prosecution's theory of the case, according to Dugan, was that Clark felt protective toward the work group. He thought Whooper was spending too much time with the women in Clark's work group, was "coming onto" or flirting with them, or maybe was becoming popular with them. Clark feared the loss of affection from the work group and the friendly relations he enjoyed. He had Whooper investigated because he wanted to find some wrongdoing by Whooper. He did not want just to harm Whooper physically but wanted him out of the workplace because of his impact on Clark's world, his "comfort zone" on his shift. Whooper was a threat because he changed the balance of relations in Clark's social world at the Postal Service. The prosecution's theory did not offer an interpretation of Clark's statement to Windle that his supervisor "singled him out," and does not address whether Clark may have feared the loss of his job, around which his life revolved.

Postal Service Workplace Violence Policies

The Postal Service has implemented three workplace violence policies on a district-by-district basis. The zero tolerance policy, adopted in 1992, acknowledged that in some settings there is an unacceptable level of stress. In warning of no tolerance for violence, threats of violence, harassment, intimidation, or bullying, the policy stated that the "need to serve the public efficiently and productively, and the need for all employees to be committed to giving a fair day's work for a fair day's pay, does not justify actions that are abusive or intolerant. *'Making the numbers' is not an excuse for the abuse of anyone.* Those who do not treat others with dignity and respect will not be rewarded or promoted. Those whose unacceptable behavior continues will be removed from their positions."

The six-strategy violence prevention program was adopted in 1994 and was coordinated through the national employee relations function. The strategies were (1) selection (screening of applicants); (2) security (varies by location, ranging from awareness and training programs to provision of security guards, surveillance cameras, and access badges); (3) policy (ban on weapons, no tolerance of threats, early intervention), (4) climate (employee opinion surveys, use of intervention teams to improve the climate, improved grievance process, management training on such issues as employee empowerment, conflict resolution, and positive reinforcement); (5) employee support (improved employee assistance program, hot line for reporting threats or concerns); and (6) separation (improved dismissal procedures, predismissal assessment of employee dangerousness). Workplace violence training had been provided to over 50,000 managers, supervisors, officials, and postmasters.

The "no firearms" policy, adopted in August 1995, referred to the shooting in California one month before, that is, the shooting of Whooper by Clark. Citing law and policy prohibiting possession of a firearm within postal installations, the policy declared that such possession is cause for summary dismissal.

In Congressional testimony in 1993, Postmaster General Marvin Runyon reported that, among other violence prevention activities, the Postal Service formed a national task force on workplace violence, which included union representatives; consulted with behavioral scientists; attended academies on workplace violence; doubled the amount of time devoted to threats and assaults; conducted a study of threats and assaults to identify common factors; developed new preemployment screening techniques; and expanded the employee assistance program to include broader issues than substance abuse, provide more and better qualified counselors, and improve the referral process.[6]

Local protocols (policies) at the City of Industry facility for preventing workplace violence provide detailed information on warning signs, threat assessment, and the role of the threat assessment team. The team is composed of managers from the areas of human resources, labor relations, the employee assistance program, safety and health, medical services, injury compensation, security, operations, and maintenance. Whooper completed four hours of supervisory training on workplace violence in February 1994, when he was assigned to the Rosemead facility. In January 1996, the Santa Ana Postal District increased the amount of training to eight hours, with training conducted by postal employees rather than an outside consultant. The collective bargaining agreement among the Postal Service and the APWU and National Association of Letter Carriers, which governed the facility, contained a section that provides for labor-management cooperation in the area of safety and health.

Questions for Discussion

1. Could the killing of James Whooper by Bruce Clark have been prevented? Explain why or why not. Be sure to address the issues of changes in management, warning signs of potential violence, and security at the City of Industry postal facility. Were Postal Service workplace violence policies effective in this case?

2. Review the composition of the threat assessment team at the City of Industry postal facility. Why is the team composed of members from different functional areas of management? The threat assessment process sometimes requires management to consult with mental health professionals. What are the implications of such collaborations? Finally, what risks are present in the administration of threat reporting and assessment procedures?

3. Predictions by mental health professionals of violent behavior by individuals are accurate in perhaps 30 percent of the cases. What are the implications for management of the difficulty in predicting workplace violence?

Violence at the United States Postal Service:

The Killing of James Whooper by Bruce Clark (B)

The Postal Service is the country's largest employer. In 1994, the Postal Service employed more than 800,000 workers at 352 mail processing and distribution plants and 39,392 post offices, branches, and stations in 85 districts. In 1997, Lasseter documented 21 cases of workplace violence at the Postal Service from 1983 to 1996, which resulted in the death of 40 postal workers and other victims; at least three additional cases have occurred since 1996.[7] In 1998, a commission was appointed to review violence and safety issues at the Postal Service.[8]

A 1994 report by the National Institute of Occupational Safety and Health, of the U.S. Centers for Disease Control and Prevention,[9] found that (1) neither the postal industry nor postal occupations were among the groups at greater risk for workplace homicide for the period 1983–1989; (2) the occupational fatality rate for postal workers was about 2.5 times lower than that for all workers combined; and (3) the homicide rate for postal workers was about the same as the national rate for all industries for the period 1983–1993 (revised figures). In 1983 to 1993, however, whereas homicide was the third leading cause of job-related death for all industries, homicide was the second leading cause of postal worker deaths on the job. Also, more coworkers have been killed at the Postal Service than in other industries.

In 1992, the Committee on Post Office and Civil Service of the U.S. House of Representatives issued a report of its investigation of the 1991 shootings at the Royal Oak, Michigan, post office, where postal worker Thomas McIlvane killed four supervisors, wounded four other employees, and committed suicide. The report cited numerous Congressional hearings and U.S. General Accounting Office (GAO) reports on postal management practices. These oversight activities repeatedly revealed the existence of an autocratic management style, which was acknowledged by Anthony M. Frank, former Postmaster General (1988–1992), on his departure. Frank said that one of his regrets was his inability to overhaul the corporate culture. He described the agency as having a "paramilitary character," wherein the question "Why do I have to do that?" often receives the answer "Because I told you to." Although improvements have been made, he said that the attitude that "I ate dirt for 20 years, now it's your turn to eat dirt," still existed among too many supervisors.[10] In testimony before Congress in 1992, Moe Biller, president of the National Rural Letter Carriers, declared that all 19 Postmasters General under whom he had served, including the incumbent, Marvin Runyon, had said that the military approach to management was at an end at the Postal Service.[11]

The Postal Service became an independent governmental organization under the terms of the Postal Reorganization Act of 1970. A 1994 GAO report on Postal Service labor-management relations noted its accomplishments in modernizing operations, improving employee compensation, forgoing direct taxpayer subsidies, and maintaining universal service. Also, the report complemented Postmaster General Runyon on his efforts to implement initiatives to help build a labor-management partnership at the national level, and to make the Postal Service a more customer-driven and employee-oriented organization.[12]

In Congressional testimony in 1993, Runyon cited the following initiatives in the area of labor-management relations: including representatives of unions and management associations in weekly senior leadership meetings at headquarters and major facilities across the country; conducting employee opinion surveys to measure factors related to employee commitment; holding managers and supervisors accountable for improving employee commitment; measuring executive performance through the process called "360-degree feedback," which utilizes assessments by supervisors, peers, and subordinates; and attempting to award advancement only to executives with "people skills."

The GAO report concluded, however, that programs since 1982 to improve workfloor relations have not changed underlying management values or systems affecting supervisor-employee relationships: "Employees continue to work in vast mail processing plants and in post offices throughout the country under a highly structured system of work rules and a highly autocratic management style." In essence, no "clear framework or strategy exists for moving agreed-upon values and principles down to first-line supervisors and employees working at processing plants and post offices."

Key findings included the existence of long-term adversarial labor relations between management and three of the four postal worker unions; inadequate performance management systems; "tense and confrontational" relations in mail processing plants, which are described as factories; and reliance on disciplinary processes and grievance procedures for conflict resolution. In 1992, a backlog of 38,335 grievance cases awaited resolution through arbitration; many employees could expect to wait a year or more for an arbitration resolution if cases continue to be processed at the 1992 rate. The cost of the grievance process for fiscal year 1992 alone was estimated at $200 million.

A 1997 GAO report declared that little progress had been made since the 1994 report was issued.[13] Adversarial relations between the Postal Service and three unions continued during the 1994 negotiations. Between fiscal years 1994 and 1996, the number of grievances rose from 65,062 to 89,931, an increase of about 38 percent, while the number of backlogged grievances rose from 36,669 to 69,555, an increase of about 90 percent. In general, the parties blamed each other for the higher volume of grievances and large number of backlogged grievances. Also, the Postal Service and the four postal worker unions and three management associations were unable to convene a labor-management relations summit.

Notably, Kinney's book on workplace violence classified the Postal Service as a "sick" workplace, a category characterized by chronic labor-management disputes; frequent employee grievances; an extraordinary number of injury claims, particularly stress claims; understaffing and/or excessive demands for overtime; a high number of stressed personnel; and an authoritarian management approach.[14] Kinney found substantial evidence that lethal perpetrators often came from such environments. Moreover, research by Baxter and Margavio concluded that the organizational climate is *conducive* to workplace violence, as a result of the impact on workers of mechanization, automation, and downsizing at the Postal Service since the 1980s. In summary, they suggested that a theoretical link exists between the management of change and recent homicides at the Postal Service.

> . . . [T]he degradation of labor under conditions of rapid technological and organizational change causes a form of social disorganization that provides the external conditions for outbreaks of assaultive violence. Employees are objectified, pressured, and intimidated by the authoritarian nature of scientific management. Resultant frustration and alienation weaken employee integration and commitment to the organization, which undermines traditional forms of social control. Over time, this frustration and alienation catalyze alternative meanings and patterns of behavior, including assaultive violence.[15]

Questions for Discussion

1. Do you think the general organizational climate at the Postal Service played a role in the workplace homicide at the City of Industry facility? Explain why or why not.

2. In the 1990s, according to the U.S. Department of Labor, workplace homicide became the second leading cause of death at the workplace after traffic accidents, up from third place; moreover, researchers have found that the incidence of employees killing their supervisors has doubled since the 1980s. Speculate as to possible causes of the rise in homicide at the workplace.

Footnotes

[1]Paul Johnson, "Ex-Postal Worker Gets 22 Years for Murder," *Los Angeles Times*, May 7, 1996, p. B3. In one incident in 1986, Patrick Henry Sherrill killed 14 coworkers, wounded six others, and committed suicide at the Edmond, Oklahoma, post office.

[2]Stephanie Simon and Edward J. Boyer, "Postal Worker Held in Slaying of Supervisor," *Los Angeles Times*, July 10, 1995, p. A15.

[3]Ted Johnson and John M. Glionna, "Postal Supervisor's Shooting Death Baffles Employees," *Los Angeles Times*, July 11, 1995, p. B10.

[4]Johnson, "Ex-Postal Worker Gets 22 Years for Murder," pp. B1, B3.

[5]See, generally, Johnson and Glionna, "Postal Supervisor's Shooting Death Baffles Employees," and Simon and Boyer, "Postal Worker Held in Slaying of Supervisor."

[6]Don Lasseter, *Going Postal: Madness and Mass Murder in America's Post Offices* (New York: Pinnacle Books, Kensington Publishing Corp., 1997). With respect to the three additional cases, see "Terror at Post Office Ends in Gunman's Death," *The Miami Herald*, September 3, 1997, www. miamiherald.com/archives, "Milwaukee Postal Worker Kills One, Then Self," *Milwaukee Journal Sentinel Online*, December 19, 1997, www.jsonline.com/archives, and "Denver Gunman Surrenders to Police," *Las Vegas Sun*, December 24, 1997, www.lasvegassun.com/archives.

[7]"Postal Workplace Violence Eyed," *Las Vegas Sun*, October 7, 1998, www. lasvegassun.com/archives.

[8]U.S. Centers for Disease Control and Prevention, "Occupational Injury Deaths of Postal Workers – States, 1980-1989," *Mortality and Morbidity Weekly Report*, 43, No. 32 (August 19, 1994), pp. 587+.

[9]See, generally, "Statement by Marvin Runyon, Chief Executive Officer and Postmaster General of the United States before the Joint Hearing of the Subcommittee on the Census, Statistics, and Postal Personnel and the Subcommittee on Postal Operations and Services, Committee on Post Office and Civil Service, U.S. House of Representatives, Washington, D.C.," August 5, 1993.

[10]"A Post Office Tragedy: The Shooting at Royal Oak," Report of the Committee on Post Office and Civil Service, House of Representatives, 102nd Congress, 2nd Session, June 15, 1992 (Washington, DC: U.S. Government Printing Office, 1992), p. 3.

[11]"Violence in the U.S. Postal Service," Joint Hearing before the Subcommittee on Postal Operations and Services and the Subcommittee on Postal Personnel and Modernization of the Committee on Post Office and Civil Service, House of Representatives, 102nd Congress, 2nd Session, September 15, 1992 (Washington, DC: U.S. Government Printing Office, 1993), p. 20.

[12]See, generally, *U.S. Postal Service: Labor-Management Problems Persist on the Workroom Floor*, I (Washington, DC: U.S. General Accounting Office, September, 1994).

[13]See, generally, *U.S. Postal Service: Little Progress Made in Addressing Persistent Labor-Management Problems* (Washington, DC: U.S. General Accounting Office), November 4, 1997.

[14]Joseph A. Kinney, *Violence at Work: How to Make Your Company Safer for Employees and Customers* (Englewood Cliffs, NJ: Prentice Hall, 1995), p. 42; see pp. 41–43.

[15]Vern Baxter and Anthony Margavio, "Assaultive Violence in the U.S. Post Office," *Work and Occupations*, 23, No. 3 (August 1996), pp. 278–279; see, generally, pp. 277–296.

When Worlds Collide

by Russell Aebig

Petr, vice president in charge of mergers and acquisitions, sat back in his chair, thinking through the events of the last two years. Historically, Evergreen, one of the largest commercial printers in America, had always been able to address strategic issues deftly, but something had gone wrong in this case. The newly formed electronic forms division was losing money with no end in sight. This was not the Evergreen way.

Situational Background

In 1993, Evergreen was faced with a dilemma. Many of its key customers were looking for a transition strategy for their business forms. In the customers' view, a migration path was needed to move from the preprinted paper forms Evergreen was printing and storing to electronic forms that would integrate with their business processes. In one respect, this would mean a decline in revenue for the Evergreen business form division. In another respect, providing this transition would lead to several lucrative contracts, including the immediate prospect of recovering a $15 million contract with a former customer.

Petr knew he had carefully assessed the situation. In addressing this need of electronic forms, it became clear that this was a significant trend for the future. Meeting the trend early would give Evergreen a significant competitive advantage. Petr also found that this trend was not seriously impacting its high-margin business forms but would transition its customers' low-margin, high-cost business forms to a low-cost electronic format, providing another reason to pursue the electronic forms opportunity.

It was clear to Petr that if these trends were to continue, getting ahead of the curve would provide a competitive advantage. How to get to market quickly was Petr's challenge. Acquiring or allying with an existing electronic forms company would provide the necessary speed to market, but there were few electronic forms packages on the market at the time. The leading electronic forms package was examined very closely as to a possible alliance to fill this need. It was determined this package would not be a good fit for Evergreen because of the following reasons:

- Evergreen would not have control over the product. As customization had to be done for individual customers, Evergreen would either be at the vendor's mercy or would not be able to meet the needs of the customer.
- The product was targeted at the retail market and not seen as a commercial product viable to be deployed across an enterprise. This was seen as a significant detriment, as Evergreen's customer base was primarily *Fortune* 1000 companies.
- In the evaluation of the product, many defects were identified. Evergreen could not go to its customers with a product containing defects.

For these reasons, Petr was determined to present Evergreen's customers with a solution that allowed them to transition from paper-based forms to electronic forms, and to do so in a manner in which Evergreen would retain control of the software. The primary position Petr presented to Evergreen's customers was a transition strategy and products to follow.

The ultimate solution was to provide a product that would access any database a customer may have, work on any workstation a customer may have, and have all the features that were available in the packages currently on the market. Aggressive goals, to be sure.

Thinking logically, Petr was clear that it was sound. Hindsight being twenty-twenty, he needed to understand what had happened.

Evergreen

Evergreen was a large business printing company with annual revenues in excess of $800 million.[1] There were four main areas of products that Evergreen provided to the business world.

The largest segment of Evergreen's operation was the manufacturing of business forms. Examples of this included monthly billing statements, credit card statements, mortgage applications, and air freight package forms. The industry's growth level was shrinking due to the apprehension in continuing to have forms preprinted on paper while electronic forms were on the horizon. Despite this, Evergreen's business forms were growing at 15 percent annually.

Line of Business	Evergreen Revenue (%)	Evergreen Growth (%)	Industry Growth (%)
Business Forms	38	15	-2.5
Direct Response	25	36	5.4
Office Products	23	12	19
Labels	14	15	8

Direct-response printing was the second largest component of Evergreen's business. Examples of this included the sweepstakes packages sent in the mail, product catalogs, health care plan directories, business solicitation mailings, and credit card offers. Office products such as legal pads, computer paper, ink jet cartridges, ATM paper rolls, and brand-name office supplies made available to its corporate customers directly comprised the third segment. The final segment was the label division. This division produced bar-coded shipping labels, consumer product labels, blank stock labels, airline bag tags, and other similar labels.

From the perspective of performance relative to the industry, it was clear that Evergreen had been very successful in each area it moved into. This success was attributed to working closely with the existing and prospective customer base to not take orders only, but to listen to their needs and develop custom solutions to each customer's unique problems.

Petr knew that much of Evergreen's success could be attributed to relationship building. Through a 700-person sales force, and the relationships established between Evergreen and its customers, Evergreen was able to understand and anticipate the needs of its customers better than the competition. Through the same type of relationship building with paper suppliers, Evergreen was able to gain competitive cost advantages for its raw materials in ways that its competition could not.

External Environment

Petr knew the constituent divisions of Evergreen exceptionally well, and instinctively knew the answer to his problem was not there. Evergreen's external environment was relatively simple, with the major variable being the cost and source of paper. This was controlled through relationships with a variety of paper suppliers and contractual obligations with the customer base. Other external variables were printer technology and customer needs.

Elements in the external environment were relatively stable. There was low uncertainty in the technology. Printing presses and commercial printers had adapted to needs over the

[1]All revenue and growth figures (Evergreen and industry average) based on Evergreen's 1996 Annual Report.

decades, but these changes were relatively slow. This, combined with few printer and press vendors, made the certainty level high for the technology. The source and cost of paper as a raw material were also stable. While the paper costs may fluctuate, the prices charged Evergreen customers were indexed to this price, resulting in a zero net change in profit ratio for Evergreen. The combination of a simple and stable environment provided a low level of uncertainty in operations.

Organization Structure

Petr felt he had to examine several aspects of Evergreen's business. Examining Evergreen's organization, it could clearly be delineated into three distinct areas.

The driving force behind Evergreen was the sales force. Evergreen had 700 salespeople who were in constant contact with their accounts (primarily *Fortune* 1000 companies). These salespeople worked very closely with the customers to identify their needs. They were trained to gather as much information as possible and then find a way to satisfy those needs. This usually meant going to more experienced sales managers for advice, and occasionally bringing in technical resources to resolve in-depth technical issues. The primary goal of the sales force was customer satisfaction.

The other major group within Evergreen was the personnel in the manufacturing plants. Evergreen had several plants distributed in various geographic regions across the United States. Each plant had a variety of printers to accommodate regional needs. The focus of the people in the manufacturing plants was to produce the products as efficiently as possible. The decision making for the plant manager was oriented around the best printer or press to use in manufacturing a product based on press availability, date needed, and efficiencies of operation.

Evergreen had a small division (less than 1 percent of employee population) that was charged with research and development. These people monitored the printer and press manufacturers for industry improvements, and the changes in technology. They would also, on occasion, rewrite software to improve performance of a particular printer, or take several printer technologies and use them in concert to provide a specific customer solution. An example of the work they do would be the improvement in quality assurance provided to customers through creative uses of bar-code technology. This service level was greater than what Evergreen's competitors could provide, and as such had been marketed as a service offering. The goals of the R&D division were to monitor new developments in the printer industry.

In working for custom solutions for customers, a few people were brought together to design the prototype product to be produced, and from this point forward, a large batch model was followed. In many cases products were also inventoried for later use to fill future orders.

Culture

Petr was very proud of the culture of Evergreen. "Find a Way to Say Yes!" summed up much of the Evergreen culture. The customer was of paramount importance and finding a way to satisfy the needs of the customer was critical to Evergreen's success. This statement was so embedded in the culture that large banners with the saying hung on the walls of many of the manufacturing plants.

Evergreen also prided itself on its independence. The employees were very loyal by industry standards and were proud to be with Evergreen. Evergreen was not the largest company in the industry, but they saw themselves as the best company.

Software Product Development

Petr had hired Jon to take over the newly formed division and called him into his office to discuss the division. More specifically, what the division was all about—developing a software product—as this was a very different process compared to producing traditional Evergreen products.

With Jon understandably concerned over being called into the vice president's office, Petr asked him, "If you were to summarize the art of software development into the basic components, what would they be?"

Thinking carefully about how to respond, Jon carefully structured his answer into inputs, outputs, and the processing that converted one into the other.

"The inputs to software development are a fixed set of requirements, a customer (or focus group) who works with the development group to provide controls throughout the development process, highly skilled technologists, and a complex methodology for delivering software."

Jon continued, "The output of the development process is a software product. In Evergreen's situation, this software was to be much more complex than most. The product was to operate against multiple databases on the back end, operate on several operating systems, and retain the features of currently available electronic forms software. In the software development industry, one operating system is typically chosen, and one database is selected for the data repository. The goal for Evergreen, therefore, was much more challenging than what would be considered the norm for the software development industry. The transformation of the inputs to outputs is based on a sophisticated methodology of developing software and a set of software tools that require highly skilled people to operate properly."

"Okay," Petr replied, "I think I understand these basics. When we produce an order for business forms, from a roll of paper, it is a much simpler process. What is the external environment for software production?"

This was the opportunity Jon was waiting for. This was the area where he was most surprised after he took over the division. "The external environment for software development is based on monitoring technology trends and products. There are several areas of technology to monitor and each of them is changing very rapidly."

While Petr was thinking through the implications of this, Jon was quick to add, "The technology for the customers' environments must also be monitored. Because the product would have to integrate with any possible configuration the customer may have in place, and the customer base is the *Fortune* 1000, this leaves the entire spectrum of possible software and hardware combinations." This was a very interesting element for Petr to factor into his analysis.

Evergreen's Electronic Forms Division

"Let's review the highlights of our activities to date," Petr suggested.

In 1993, Evergreen acquired a small electronic forms company for a relatively small sum of money. This company specialized in converting preprinted business forms into electronic copies that may be stored in multiple ways. The software developed for filling forms online was cryptic by industry standards, but it did meet the minimal needs of the industry.

In order to meet the expectations of the customer base, this acquisition was brought into the Evergreen organization as its own division. The owners of the acquired company had billed electronic forms as having greater revenues than the rest of the company combined in a few years. Based on this, Evergreen structured the division as a profit center that was fully accountable for not only its own costs but its share of the corporate overhead.

"Those were the days of optimism," piped in Jon. "I remember the view we had internally, as well as how our customers felt."

The customer view of the new division was mixed. The general view was that this new division was able to provide the direction toward electronic forms they were looking for. The software being put forth in this area was unsatisfactory, however. As a new division, it was felt this product would evolve into a more robust—an industry standard—software product, which would be acceptable within the organization.

Petr wanted to bring the focus back to the management of the division. "We felt the existing management of the acquisition would not be able to achieve the results we wanted, so we brought it inside and assigned you to run it—the Evergreen way. You were a senior sales manager with 15 years with the company. You had contacts within all our major accounts in addition to knowing everyone within Evergreen."

Petr continued, "I understood that you needed help on the technical side so we hired a technical manager from outside the company to manage the day-to-day operations of the division."

Jon knew that Petr was right. Petr had given him the tools needed to succeed. The new manager provided the organization with the technical management experience necessary to deliver the product. With his experience within the organization and in the customer base, the combination was seen as being the best of both worlds.

Several actions were taken once the new management took control. Several products that provided little benefit were discontinued, a focus was mandated to create the long-term solution for the customer base, and staffing was started to support these efforts.

The marriage was not perfect, however. Several problems began to emerge within the division.

- Once the new product became a focus, the analysis of exactly what was to be produced took place. The estimates of the effort required to produce this product was three to four times greater than the Evergreen executive had expected. Being a sales-driven organization, with a relatively short time horizon, the additional time required was seen as being unacceptable and had to be pared down. Jon particularly had difficulty with this long time horizon.

- Evergreen had always been a customer-driven company. In working with customers closely, Evergreen had always been able to find solutions to unique problems the customer may have. This was easier to do when the number of variables was limited to the printer and press technologies available. This was much more difficult when dealing with the many possible variations of hardware and software that a *Fortune* 1000 company may have had within its organization. The inability to meet these demands immediately caused a problem with Petr.

- The sales force was having a difficult time selling the product and services of electronic forms. The sales force was used to selling paper forms, labels, and office products. Electronic forms, and the associated technology, were foreign to them. Without the familiarity with the technology, selling it to customers became very difficult. A problem compounding this was that the sales audience for electronic forms was the MIS department, not the office supplies person they knew and frequently contacted. Not only was this a different person, but they also spoke a technical language the sales force had a difficult time understanding.

- The reward structure of the sales force was counter to selling electronic forms. The sales force was given incentives for each sale. By selling electronic forms, they would not have any repeat sales for these forms. As a result they saw no value in pushing a product that would not benefit them.

- Being customer oriented, the technical personnel who were to develop the new product were constantly being pulled off the project to work on presales support for the sales force. This was necessary as the sales force was unable to communicate with the MIS departments within the customer base.
- The staffing of the division was challenging from the standpoint of the type of people required for the job, and the impression these people would have of working for a manufacturing company. The required personnel for the new division were to be professional. Professional people typically wish to work for professional firms. Manufacturing firms are not usually seen as being high on the selected list for professionals.

While these problems were not insurmountable, they pointed to a fundamental problem. What was the problem Petr needed to solve? What should he have done differently to avoid the problems he was currently facing? What could he do at this time to rectify the situation?

NOTES

NOTES

NOTES

NOTES

NOTES

NOTES

NOTES

NOTES